# HIP CLASSES

CHG        KYNDA CG

KARA CG

MOD KILDIN DD        KANIN DDG

AK I FFG        ALESHA MCS        RIGA FF

ALLIGATOR I LST        ALLIGATOR III LST

PETYA I FFL        PETYA II FFL        POLNOCNY Type A LSM

SF    NATYA MSF    OSA I PTG    OSA II PTG    POTI PG    NANUCHKA PGG

**Second Edition**

# SOVIET NAVAL
## DEVELOPMENTS

Prepared at the direction of the
Chief of Naval Operations by the
Director of Naval Intelligence
and the Chief of Information

Department of the Navy,
Washington, D.C.

# Foreword by Norman Polmar

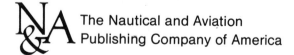
The Nautical and Aviation
Publishing Company of America

**Library of Congress Cataloging in Publication Data**
Main entry under title:

Soviet naval developments.

    1. Soviet Union. Voenno-Morskoi flot.
2. Merchant marine--Soviet Union. 3. Sea-power
--Soviet Union. I. United States. Office of
Naval Intelligence. II. United States. Navy
Dept. Office of the Chief of Information.
VA573.S567 1981    359ˢ.00947    81-14104
ISBN 0-933852-24-X        AACR2

# Foreword

The idea for this work originated a decade ago, in discussions with the Director of Naval Intelligence and Chief of Information, as a means of providing U.S. naval officers with an unclassified synopsis of Soviet naval developments. At that time, the first manifestations of a new phase in Soviet naval activity were becoming evident: the supersonic Backfire strike aircraft was about to enter Soviet naval service; the first DELTA-class submarines with their 4,000-mile missile were being completed; a strange submarine, given the code name ALFA, had just emerged from the Sudomekh yard at Leningrad; and the huge warship being built at Nikolayev near the Black Sea was identified as the Soviet Union's first "aircraft carrier," the KIEV.

There were other activities taking place as well, some readily apparent to the perceptive reader of the open press. But the message was plainly there: the Soviet Navy was embarking on still another phase of development with surface ships, submarines, aircraft, satellite systems and other hardware that presaged a new understanding of the role of the sea power in the last two decades of this century and the beginning of the 21st century.

This latest edition of this now widely read and used work describes the further manifestations of that phase. The most obvious features are, of course, the warships and aircraft, which can be easily observed and described in these pages. But keeping apace with the visible hardware have been significant improvements in Soviet Command, Control, and Communications ($C^3$); the Soviet Ocean Surveillance System (SOSS); anti-ship and anti-submarine weaponry, including mines; fire control, radar, and sonar systems; probably non-acoustic submarine detection capabilities; and, of course, operational tactics and doctrine.

Indeed, tactics and doctrine, which for a number of reasons receive scant space in this volume, are perhaps the most difficult aspects of Soviet naval developments to divine, for not only is Soviet military-naval hardware

"different" than their counterparts in the Western navies, but they will be employed differently.

These tactics and doctrine are intended to effectively carry out the wartime missions of the Soviet Navy, which can be broadly listed as:

1. Strategic nuclear strike
2. Destruction of Western strike forces (missile submarines, aircraft carriers, amphibious ships)
3. Destruction of Western merchant shipping
4. Support of ground force operations
5. Protection of merchant shipping

The forces developed to carry out these wartime missions are available in peacetime to support the state interests of the Soviet Union. During the past decade Soviet naval forces have been employed in crisis management, latent imposition, logistic support of allies and "clients," and political pressure. Some or all of these peacetime activities could be grouped under the heading "gunboat diplomacy." Despite its archaic sound, gunboat diplomacy is still practiced in the last quarter of the 20th century as much as the world continues to be dependent upon the sea for its political, economic, and military well-being.

This volume provides descriptions of several warships that had not yet gone to sea when the previous edition was published, especially the nuclear-propelled cruiser KIROV. This ship in many ways symbolizes the current phase of Soviet naval development. In the Soviet tradition the KIROV is large and innovative. At 23,000 tons full-load displacement, the KIROV is the largest warship built by any navy since World War II except for aircraft carriers. She is highly original with respect to her weapons and electronics, some of which had not been previously seen on Soviet warships, demonstrating the continued development of combat systems in the Soviet Navy as well as new platforms to carry them. The KIROV also introduces nuclear propulsion to Soviet surface warships, although three civilian-operated icebreakers as well as about 180 submarines with nuclear propulsion had previously been constructed.* Even here the Soviet Navy has broken new ground, with the KIROV having an advanced combination conventional steam-nuclear steam plant, probably providing the advantages of both systems in a single plant with some savings in costs and nuclear-trained personnel compared to an all-nuclear powered ship.

And even the KIROV may be the harbinger of still other Soviet developments in this phase of soviet naval activities, with a nuclear-propelled aircraft carrier of perhaps 60,000 tons reported to be under construction at the Black Sea Shipyard in Nikolayev.

Norman Polmar
*September 1, 1981*

*\*One nuclear submarine was accidentally lost in 1970, and several early units have been laid up in reserve.*

## Publisher's Note

Mr. Polmar is an internationally known author, analyst, and historian, specializing in U.S. and Soviet naval and strategic issues. In 1974, at the request of the U.S. Navy's Director of Naval Intelligence and Chief of Information, Mr. Polmar compiled and edited the first edition of this work. Subsequently, the Navy asked him to prepare the Navy's third edition, the first to be published in a revised trade edition.

## Acknowledgement

It would be a long list if all the persons who contributed to the publishing of this book were personally recognized. I would particularly like to thank those analysts and desk officers of the Office of Naval intelligence; Naval Intelligence Command and its field activities; and the Defense Intelligence Agency's Directorate for Research who assisted me in researching and writing both this edition, as well as the earlier edition of *Soviet Naval Developments*. Additionally, a number of persons in the office of Naval Information; Naval Publications Branch; Department of Defense's Directorate for Freedom of Information and Security Review and the Government Printing Office provided extraordinary contributions to the production and publication of this book.

Captain William H. Cracknell, USN
Editor

# Table of Contents

# Section 1. Purpose

*The Soviet Navy has been transformed into an important strategic force, into a force capable of opposing aggression from the sea and accomplishing major operational and strategic missions on the World Ocean. . . . Its relative weight within the composition of the (Soviet) armed forces is continually increasing. . . .*

Admiral of the Fleet of the Soviet Union
S.G. GORSHKOV

One of the most dramatic developments of the post-World War II period has been the growth of Soviet naval and maritime activities.* Today the Soviet Union is a true "sea power" challenging United States in all aspects of maritime activity. From the end of World War II until the early 1970s the United States maintained unquestioned naval supremacy. This gave the United States great flexibility in foreign policy and provided one of the West's primary shields against Soviet aggression.

During much of this period the Soviet Navy—except for submarines—was ranked fourth after the U.S., British, and French navies. Only in numbers of submarines could the Soviet Navy rank as a leader at sea in the early post-war era, reaching a peak of some 450 diesel submarines in 1958. Although the Soviet Navy had quantitative superiority in undersea craft, there were substantial qualitative shortcomings in equipment, personnel, and leadership. Further, Soviet surface warships and submarines seldom ventured far from the coasts of the U.S.S.R.

Today, after a great expenditure of resources, the Soviet Navy has achieved quantitative and qualitative leadership is several aspects of naval power. This Soviet leadership, both real and perceived, is having considerable impact on international political, economic, ideological, and military developments.

Accordingly, it is important for U.S. Navy personnel to be professionally knowledgeable about the Soviet Navy and its development. Further, it is not enough that just we in the Navy understand Soviet naval developments. We must also assist in illuminating the issues for the American public about this unprecedented peacetime expansion of naval power. This Fourth Edition of *Understanding Soviet Naval Developments* is intended to provide the necessary background information for naval personnel to discuss the Soviet Navy intelligently both internally and in public forums.

There is a tendency in some quarters to foster scenarios which place the Soviet Navy in the best light while placing the U.S. Navy in "worst case" situations. This approach is alarmist and misleading, just as the position that all Soviet naval developments are strictly defensive or are merely a reaction to U.S. and other NATO actions, is complacent and misleading. The Soviet Navy is inferior in several important respects to the U.S. Navy; it has problems and limitations as has the military service of any nation. These will be discussed later in the text.

The considerable influence that the Soviet Navy exerts in world affairs today can be traced to the great strides that it has made in technology, production, operations, and tactics, as well as its extensive use as an instrument of Soviet foreign policy. These developments are of major concern to the U.S. Navy because they narrow the options open to the United States in a crisis situation, and because they could result in confrontations with the Soviet Navy or with other navies which employ Soviet weapons and tactics.

This publication discusses the expansion of Soviet maritime strength from its beginnings to its present status and the trends which are indicated for the future. The manual has been published for the widest dissemination within the Navy.

---

*In this context, "maritime activities" includes the merchant marine, fishing industry, research and shipbuilding activities.*

1

The Tsarist Russian battleship RETVIZAN's visit to New York in 1901 gave Americans one of their few looks at Russian naval forces. Some American perceptions of Russian naval developments may date back to the RETVIZAN and her participation in the Russo-Japanese War of 1904–1905, a Russian disaster. In the foreground is the U.S. submarine HOLLAND.

The nuclear powered missile cruiser KIROV is a symbol of the rash of new classes of warships and submarines which the Soviets will be adding to their fleet in the decade of the eighties—larger with more sophisticated weapons and sensors than their impressive predecessors. KIROV is the Soviets' first nuclear powered warship and is the largest warship (less carriers) built by any navy since the end of World War II.

# Section 2. Soviet Naval Policy

*The flag of the Soviet Navy flies over the oceans of the world. Sooner or later the United States will have to understand it no longer has mastery of the seas.*

*Admiral of the Fleet of the Soviet Union*
*S.G. GORSHKOV*

Soviet naval policy is based on a Russian drive to extend national influence by maritime activities, a drive which dates back almost 300 years. This effort has continued, with varying emphasis, under the Tsars, and the commissars who followed them. Sometimes spearheaded by explorers and researchers, at times by the merchant fishing fleets, often by the navy, this effort is now being made by a combination of all of these maritime forces on a scale without precedent.

## A. Perspective, 1700–1953

The Soviet Navy traces its beginnings from the early 1700s when the Western-oriented Tsar Peter I founded a city (now Leningrad) on the Neva marshes at the eastern end of the Gulf of Finland and built a navy to fight the Swedes. Prior to that time the only secure Russion outlet to the sea was on the frigid Arctic coast. Employing British and Dutch shipbuilders and officers, Peter constructed a fleet which achieved major victories against the enemy, and established Russia as a power in the Baltic region. Later, America's naval hero of the Revolution, John Paul Jones, served as an admiral in the Russian Navy during the reign of Catherine the Great.

During the centuries that followed, Tsarist, and then Soviet, naval forces had few victories at sea of which to boast. Although there were some decisive triumphs against the Turks in the 18th and 19th centuries, British and French naval forces present in the Mediterranean and elsewhere, frustrated Russian ambitions.

The overwhelming defeats inflicted on Russian fleets by the Japanese Navy in the war of 1904–1905 dramatically demonstrated the former's shortcomings—a lack of preparedness, poor coordination,

and an inability to sustain prolonged operations on the high seas far from home ports. A decade later, in World War I, the Russian Navy was ineffective in the conflict against Germany, a cause for disillusionment among the sailors who later became the torchbearers of the second, or Bolshevik, revolution in the fall of 1917.

The revolutions and the civil war that followed had destroyed the navy and other maritime resources, including shipbuilding. Among other things, the "torchbearer" sailors, whose cooperation had been crucial to the success of the Bolshevik revolution, turned against the government in an open revolt at Kronstadt in March 1921 demanding an end to Communist Party dictatorship, political freedom and civil rights. Needless to say, the Soviet authorities put down the revolt by shooting some of the former heroes and imprisoning others. Yet today, this nasty incident is all but forgotten and the men of the Navy are held in high esteem by the Soviet government.

Not until extensive shipyard expansion in the early 1930s could the Soviets begin construction of large submarines and destroyers. Although several cruisers and battleships were begun on the eve of World War II, only a few were completed and those that were available contributed little to the outcome of the conflict.

Interestingly enough, the way having been paved for World War II by a hastily concluded Soviet-German friendship pact, the Soviets had the world's largest submarine fleet. There were 165 Soviet submarines compared to 57 in the German Navy, and 95 in the U.S. Navy. When the Soviet Union entered the war in June 1941 they had 218 submarines. Yet these undersea craft enjoyed few successes, and had no impact on the course of the war due to geographic limitations and climatic conditions which often left them ice-bound in the Baltic. Poor training, outmoded tactics, and an inability to cope with German mines and other antisubmarine forces further neutralized the Soviet undersea fleet. Thus, the Soviet Navy played only a minor, supporting role in the conflict. It was the massive Soviet Army which won the great battles that contributed significantly to the defeat of Hitler's Germany. And it was the Army which remained as the Soviet Union's threat to the war-ravaged nations of Eastern and Western Europe after the war had ended. As peace came the Soviet Union again was incapable of building a major fleet; one-third of the country had been overrun by German armies and 20 million persons—ten percent of the population—had either been killed in battle or had died of privation.

Still, Joseph Stalin, the Soviet dictator, sought an ocean-going navy for the Soviet Union. High priorities were given to this task and by the late 1940s, the nation's shipbuilding industry had been rebuilt sufficiently (in part by using German technology and engineers) to begin work on submarines, battleships, cruisers and destroyers. Even construction of aircraft carriers was planned, but Stalin died in March 1953 and his schemes for an oceangoing fleet were buried with him. In the months that followed the dictator's death, shipbuilding programs were cancelled or cut back. For example, only 14 of 24 projected SVERDLOV class light cruisers were completed; none of the larger STALINGRAD class cruisers or pre-war SOVIET UNION class battleships was finished and the carrier program did not get past the drawing board.

## B. Khrushchev's Policies

Nikita Khrushchev, when he emerged as the new ruler of the Kremlin, initiated new policies affecting the size and composition of the Soviet Navy. In 1956, he appointed Sergei Gorshkov, a 45 year-old naval officer who had attained the rank of rear admiral at the age of 31 to be Commander-in-Chief of the Soviet Navy and directed him to dismantle the larger surface warships. Khrushchev's point-of-view in this regard, is reflected in a remark attributed to him that large warships were only useful for hauling around admirals. As a consequence, Admiral Gorshkov presided over the dismantling of much of Stalin's big-ship navy. Existing battleships were scrapped, as were several older cruisers and destroyers. Many personnel were either retired or dismissed; and all of the several thousand land-based fighter aircraft of the Soviet Navy were transferred to the National Air Defense Forces.**

In the place of Stalin's planned ocean-going fleet,

Admiral Gorshkov was directed to develop a missile-armed navy of small craft and submarines which could "defend the Soviet Union from possible Western aggression." It was hoped that comparatively inexpensive guided (cruise) missiles could counter the U.S. naval forces which were then being augmented during the Korean War (1950–1953). Soviet military planners were particularly concerned with U.S. aircraft carriers which could launch planes carrying nuclear bombs against their homeland while several hundred miles at sea, and with amphibious forces which could land troops on the Soviet coasts.

During the 1950s the Soviet Navy developed destroyers and submarines that could fire against U.S. aircraft carriers while the Soviet ships remained under the protection of land-based fighter aircraft. For coastal defense, the Soviets built the famed KOMAR and then OSA classes of missile boats which were armed with STYX (SS-N-2) antiship missiles. Also, several hundred medium bombers were transferred to Soviet Naval Aviation for use against ships and submarines.

By the late 1950s Admiral Gorshkov was able to obtain approval for larger missile-firing ships. The first of these were the KYNDA class cruisers. Each has eight launching tubes plus eight reloads for the SS-N-3 antiship missile. With target acquisition provided by either an aircraft, a submarine, or a surface ship, the missile can deliver up to a ton of high explosives or a nuclear warhead against hostile ships some 250 miles away.

This concern for countering aircraft carriers was intense during the 1950s and 1960s and substantial resources were dedicated to this task. Although in recent years the strategic missile submarine force and antisubmarine warfare (ASW) received greater emphasis, the Soviet Navy still maintains extensive and formidable anticarrier forces. The latest weapon system assigned to this task is the supersonic BACKFIRE bomber, and several new missile and ship designs appear to be primarily intended for the antiship role.

Soviet concern about the U.S. Navy, centered on the strategic striking power of carrier-based aircraft, assumed a new dimension in 1960 when the first U.S. ballistic missile submarine, GEORGE WASHINGTON, went to sea carrying 16 POLARIS strategic missiles. Forty-one U.S. nuclear powered,

---

**Since 1960 the Soviet Union has had five separate military services or forces. In their normal order of precedence they are: Strategic Rocket Forces, Ground Forces, National Air Defense Forces; Air Forces and Navy.*

ballistic missile submarines were completed from 1960 to 1967, providing a massive deterrent to Soviet aggression. Later, most of these submarines were converted to carry the longer range POSEIDON missile and twelve of these submarines are presently being back-fitted with the 4,000 mile range TRIDENT I weapon.

Response by the Soviet Navy to U.S. strategic missile submarines included construction of new classes of antisubmarine ships, among them the unusual and unique helicopter carrying missile cruisers MOSKVA and LENINGRAD. These well armed ships, described in detail in a subsequent section, each operate up to 18 ASW helicopters fitted with submarine detection devices and capable of carrying bombs or torpedoes.

The Soviet Navy under Khrushchev thus was configured as an aggressively employed defensive force, initially used for close-in coastal defense, then to attack approaching U.S. aircraft carriers and then to counter the threat from strategic missile submarines.

However, the ships, submarines and aircraft developed for these roles would be capable of carrying out other Soviet military objectives, as well as supporting political and even economic goals, particularly in peacetime. Like large navies before it, the modern Soviet fleet would prove to be a highly flexible instrument for use by that nation's leadership.

## C. The Navy Goes To Sea

Admiral Gorshkov only partially implemented Khrushchev's directives to halt big-ship building programs and dispose of many older warships. In point of fact, 14 of the SVERDLOV class light cruisers were completed during this period of upheaval. It would only be a few years later that Gorshkov, unhindered by directives to the contrary, had the Soviet Navy building large surface war ships. In the interim he pushed development of missile-armed destroyers, patrol boats and diesel submarines, as

Another significant indicator of Soviet excursions into all facets of seapower application is the recently built hospital ship, OB. This is the first new hospital ship to enter the Soviet inventory since World War II. A second, YENISEY, is expected to be completed in 1981. Both these ships were built in Poland.

An AIST air cushion landing craft moving at high speed demonstrates the Soviet Navy's attention to amphibious assault. The Soviet Naval Infantry—marine corps—is small, about 12,000 men, but well armed and carried in modern ships and landing craft.

well as nuclear powered submarines. The first of these new ships appeared in the late 1950s.

Still, Admiral Gorshkov was unable to build an ocean-going fleet except for the aforementioned submarines, and even there the Soviet Navy had operational limitations. The lack of a far-ranging fleet was politically embarrassing to the Soviet government in 1956 when Anglo-French naval forces invaded Suez, in 1958 when U.S. naval forces landed in Lebanon and in 1962 when a U.S. naval blockade (and the threat of overwhelming nuclear retaliation) forced the Soviets to withdraw strategic weapons from Cuba. In these situations the Soviets virtually had no options for countering Western political-military activities at sea except by propaganda. These lessons appear to have indelibly impressed the present leaders in the Kremlin.

In 1963 the Soviet Navy Chief "ordered his men to sea." Despite limitations in training, experience, support capabilities and the like, the Soviet Navy began operating beyond its traditional coastal areas and out of its defensive posture. By mid-1964 Soviet warships had established a continual presence in the Mediterranean. An average of five ships were maintained in the Mediterranean that year; the number gradually increased and soon Mediterranean port visits were scheduled. During the Arab-Israeli war in June 1967, a steady stream of Soviet ships passed through the Turkish Straits into the Mediterranean until the Soviet Mediterranean Squadron numbered about 70 surface warships, submarines, and support ships.

Subsequently, the Soviet Navy has maintained an average of at least 40 to 45 ships in the Mediterranean. Periodically, the number increases as relieving surface ships from the Black Sea Fleet and submarines from the Northern Fleet enter the Mediterranean (through the Strait of Gibraltar) and operate for a short period of time together with the ships they are replacing.

Soviet ability to rapidly deploy naval forces in the Mediterranean area was demonstrated in October-November 1973. Within a few days of the outbreak of hostilities in the Middle East, a steady stream of Soviet naval ships passed south through the Turkish Straits, and a second Northern Fleet submarine group entered the Mediterranean. These forces doubled the strength of the Soviet Mediterranean Squadron.

By early November, when the 1973 crisis reached its peak, there were 96 Soviet naval units in the Mediterranean: 5 cruisers, 14 destroyers, 6 patrol ships, 2 NANUCHKA class middle ships, 9 amphibious ships, 6 intelligence ships, and approximately 25 submarines (several of which were nuclear-powered); with the remainder being nearly 30 support ships. The surface ships had 20 surface-to-air missile launchers as well as a considerable number of antiship missiles. Several of the submarines also carried antiship missiles.

However, neither one of the two MOSKVA class helicopter carriers was in the Mediterranean, nor was the new KARA class cruiser NIKOLAYEV, which had left the Mediterranean on the eve of the buildup. The absence of these ships indicated that the powerful and unprecedented reinforcement of the Soviet Mediterranean Squadron was less than an all-out effort. Possibly the Soviet strategy called for withholding these primarily ASW ships at the beginning of a conflict, or they simply did not wish to risk these high-value ships in the Middle East conflict.

Still, the Soviets were able to deploy 96 surface ships and submarines into the Mediterranean during a period when the U.S. Sixth Fleet reached a peak strength of 66 ships. The three aircraft carriers then present provided the most potent U.S. conventional warfare capabilities in the region. Although Soviet Black Sea Fleet naval aircraft were within striking range of the eastern Mediterranean, they would have had to violate Turkish air-space to get there.

The only other strike aircraft in the immediate area at the time which could have been made available to the Soviets were 12 TU-22 BLINDER bombers recently delivered to Iraq. However, airfields in Egypt and Libya (including the former U.S. Wheelus Air Force Base) had, in the past, supported Soviet aircraft and could have accommodated Soviet BADGERs and BLINDERs if political permission were obtained.

In addition to the naval buildup, it is interesting to observe that very shortly after hostilities erupted between Israel and the Arab states, numerous Soviet merchant ships began loading tanks, aircraft and other war material in Black Sea ports. Most of the estimated 2,000 tanks that were supplied to the Arab armies after the outbreak of war, as well as considerable amounts of other war supplies, were transported to Egypt and Syria by Soviet merchant ships. These ships complemented the intensive Soviet airlift delivering more time-critical items such as disassembled fighter aircraft and guided missiles.

Soviet warships began operating regularly in the Indian Ocean during the late 1960s, in the Caribbean in 1969 and off the western coast of Africa late in 1970. The Kremlin leadership had discovered Sea Power!

These warships, flying the Soviet Hammer and

Admiral of the Fleet of the Soviet Union Sergey Georgi-yevich Gorschkov has been the Commander-in-Chief of the Soviet Navy since 1956. Under his leadership the navy has been transformed from a coastal defense force into a formidable global strategic force which is now a flexible instrument of Soviet foreign policy. A Great Russian born 26 February 1910, Gorshkov joined the navy in 1927, after graduation from Frunze Higher Naval School. He served in destroyers in the Black Sea and Pacific Fleets through the 1930s and was appointed Rear Admiral in 1941—right after the Germans declared war on the U.S.S.R. He distin-guished himself in several Black Sea commands during the war including the Azov and Danube Flotillas. He was commander of the Black Sea Fleet when he was picked for the Commander-in-Chief. Gorshkov also is a Deputy Minister of Defense and a Full Member of the Central Committee of the Communist Party. His "hats" make him the approximate equivalent of both the Secretary of Navy, a civilian position, and the Chief of Naval Operations in the U.S. Navy organization. Gorshkov has published a number of works; best known are his series of articles en-titled *Navies in War and Peace* and his widely distributed book, *The Sea Power of the State*, now in its second edi-tion. Gorshkov's likely successor, if he should retire in the next several years, is either Admiral of the Fleet G.M. Yegorov, Chief of Main Naval Staff, or Admiral of the Fleet N.I. Smirnov, First Deputy Commander-in-Chief.

Sickle, represent Soviet interests—economic, politi-cal and military. The Soviets are employing their navy in much the same way as the United States, Great Britain and other naval powers effectively used ships to support their national interests in var-ious parts of the world during the previous decades. In their rediscovery of the use of ships to support state interests, the capabilities of the Soviet Navy have expanded greatly, and the tasks and missions assigned to the Navy also have increased in scope and number.

## D. Expanding Naval Missions

Over the last two decades the Soviet Navy has been transformed from a basically coastal defense force into an ocean-going fleet designed to extend the defenses of the U.S.S.R. well to sea, and to per-form most of the traditional functions of a naval power in waters distant from the Soviet Union. Multi-ocean exercises, such as OKEAN-70 and 75, and the continued naval presence in distant seas, supported by the construction of larger, more pow-erful warships manifest this evolution of the role of the Soviet Navy in world affairs.

Recent Soviet military writings also reflect the evolution of naval missions. An example of this is the 1976 article on the Soviet Navy signed by Ad-miral Gorshkov in the *Soviet Military Encyclopedia,* which characterized the Navy as:

> *The branch of the armed forces intended to carry out strategic and operational missions in the sea and ocean theaters of combat op-erations. With respect to its combat capabil-ities, today's Navy is capable of delivering strikes by its strategic nuclear forces against important enemy ground targets, of destroy-ing his naval forces at sea and in their bases, of disrupting enemy ocean and sea commu-nications and protecting our own sea com-munications, and to evacuate the sick and wounded. The navy can conduct a naval op-eration both independently and jointly with other branches of the armed forces.*

By studying such writings of Soviet authors, par-ticularly Admiral Gorshkov's most recent book *Sea Power of the State* (2nd ed., revised 1978), by anal-yzing Soviet naval exercises and activity and by ob-serving the ships, aircraft and weapons built by the Soviets, a reasonable understanding of their naval missions can be determined.

According to Admiral Gorshkov, the basic mis-sion of the Soviet Navy is the "battle against the shore." He writes that:

> *In our day, a navy operating against the*

*shore possessed the capability . . . of directly affecting the course and even the outcome of the war. In this connection, naval operations against the shore have assumed dominant importance in naval warfare, and both the technical policy of building a navy and the development of the art of naval warfare have been subordinated to them.*

The "battle against the shore" is used in both the offensive and defensive sense, and includes strategic missile strikes against enemy "shore" targets, attacking the enemy's threat to one's own "shore," and supporting the ground forces. More specifically, Soviet naval missions can be stated as: (1) strategic offense, (2) maritime security of the Soviet Union, (3) interdiction of sea lines of communication, (4) support of the ground forces and, in situations short of general war, (5) the support of state policy.

## Strategic Offense

The priority given to the development of ballistic missile submarines (SSBN) over the past decade makes it clear that strategic nuclear strike capability has become a prime mission of the Soviet Navy.

From 1967 through 1979 Soviet shipyards completed 66 nuclear powered strategic missile submarines of the YANKEE and DELTA classes.

Construction of the enlarged DELTA III submarines is continuing while the initial unit of a much larger SSBN, the TYPHOON class, was launched in the fall of 1980. DELTAs, at about 13,000 tons submerged diplacement, are the world's largest submarines in service, however, the TYPHOON is estimated to be over twice the submerged displacement of the DELTA III. By comparison our OHIO class submarines, will displace more than 18,000 tons submerged and carry 24 TRIDENT Submarine-Launched Ballistic Missiles (SLBMs).

Accompanying this intensive strategic submarine development program has been a succession of improved SLBMs. The 1,300-nautical mile SS-N-6 missile originally carried by the YANKEES is being replaced with slightly longer-range variants, some carrying multiple warheads (MRV). The SS-N-8 carried by the DELTAs has a range of over 4,000 nautical miles, while the SS-N-18 missiles carried on the later DELTA variants provide increased range, more accuracy and, in some models, multiple independently targetable warheads (MIRV).

At the end of 1980 the relative strengths of the

Soviet admirals salute during a naval review as the cruiser KRASNY KAVKAZ passes. A year later, in June 1941, this fleet went to war with Nazi Germany. The contribution of the Red Navy to the war was of little significance; still, Stalin, the Soviet leader, perceived that naval power was important for the U.S.S.R. to become a world power.

U.S. and Soviet fleets in numbers of modern ballistic missile submarines and submarine launched missiles were:

Figure 1.
## BALLISTIC MISSILE SUBMARINES AND MISSILES

| | United States | Soviet Union |
|---|---|---|
| Modern Submarines (Nuclear)* | 41 | 62 |
| Older Submarines (Nuclear) | 0 | 8 |
| Older Submarines (Diesel) | 0 | about 15 |
| SLBMs | 656 | 950 + |

*The Soviets have been adhering to the total of 62 allowed under the terms of SALT I by removing the missile tubes from older YANKEEs. The U.S. is in the process of decommissioning the first of its older SSBNs in anticipation of the commissioning of new OHIO class SSBNs.

Today, U.S. submarines and strategic missiles are qualitatively superior to the Soviet weapons in several key categories; however, that qualitative advantage is being narrowed as Soviet development efforts continue at a rapid pace.

When the lead TRIDENT submarine, the USS OHIO, is delivered, the U.S. Navy will add its first new strategic missile submarine since 1967. Since that date the Soviets have completed 66 modern

Admiral Gorshkov emphasized the development of antiship missiles. By the late 1950s several missiles were at sea, including the SS-N-2 STYX. At top, Soviet sailors lower a STYX into a launch tube and, above, an OSA missile boat fires a STYX.

SSBNs and continue to construct several more each year. If the terms of SALT I are superceded by SALT II, the Soviets can elect to expand their force beyond the limit of 62.

In addition, about 15 older GOLF II (diesel) and 8 HOTEL (nuclear) ballistic missile submarines are estimated to be operational in the Soviet Navy. Although most of these submarines have shorter range and less sophisticated missiles, they do pose a threat, especially in the European theater and the western Pacific.

The large commitment of resources which the Soviet leaders have allocated to their sea-based nuclear strike forces is indicative of the vital importance of that force.

## Maritime Security

The mission of providing for the maritime security of the Soviet Union includes both strategic and tactical defense tasks to eliminate naval threats against the Soviet homeland. This is an expansion of the Navy's tradition "defense of the homeland" mission. Soviet naval forces are very aggressively and offensively oriented in exercising these "defensive" tasks; the Soviets are firm believers in the old adage, "the best defense is a good offense."

Included in the mission of maritime security is the destruction of enemy naval forces, particularly those that pose a strategic threat to the Soviet Union, such as Western strategic missile submarines and aircraft carriers. The Soviets have considerable forces available to locate and attack surface formations such as carrier and amphibious task forces. Although they have expended considerable resources in recent years on antisubmarine warfare, including an intensive ASW research and development program, it is apparent that the Soviets have not resolved the problem of locating submarines on the high seas with a high degree of probability. This task becomes progressively more difficult as longer-range missiles become available to permit submarines to operate in much larger ocean areas and still remain within range of their targets. But the Soviet ASW efforts are considerable and continuing.

Another aspect of maritime security is Soviet countering of the considerable ASW forces of the U.S. Navy and our Allies. The Soviets are thus concerned with the protection of their own SSBNs and have developed forces to attack Western ASW forces in a "defense in depth" concept. Admiral Gorshkov describes this task by noting:

*Diverse warfare ships and aircraft are included in the inventory of our Navy in order to give combat stability to the submarines and comprehensively support them, to battle the enemy's surface and ASW forces. . .*

In support of this mission, the Soviet Navy has developed several classes of large ASW ships which, along with aircraft and submarines, appear to be intended to enhance the survivability of Soviet submarines. This is a highly specialized form of "sea control". However, the newer classes of large ASW ships, especially the KRESTA II and KARA cruiser classes—are multi-purpose ships which have significant antiair warfare (AAW) and antisurface warfare (ASUW) capabilities as well. Thus, these versatile warships are suitable for use in sea control roles in addition to screening submarines. Again, operating with submarines and aircraft, the large ASW ships can permit the Soviets to exercise their own type of sea control to provide maritime security for their submarines, amphibious and merchant convoys, minelaying forces, replenishment ships, particularly in those waters considered critical by the Soviet leadership.

### Sea-Line Interdiction

The interdiction of Western sea lines of communication (SLOC) has been a mission of the Soviet Navy since the beginning of the "cold war". The relative importance of SLOC interdiction within the hierarchy of Soviet naval missions has fluctuated, depending on the current perceptions of the likely nature and length of a NATO-Warsaw Pact conflict. If such a war were nuclear and of short duration, Soviet anti-SLOC operations would be of little consequence. But since the advancement of NATO's "flexible response" strategy, as well as increased conventional and nuclear capabilities on the Soviet side, the Soviets have written more frequently about the possibilities of a conventional war and prolonged conflict.

Although the extent and timing of a SLOC interdiction campaign would depend on the nature of the initial stage of the conflict, the Soviets have clearly indicated that they regard SLOC interdiction as an important task. They have a large capability in their submarine and air forces to fight such a campaign once the decision to do so has been made. As Admiral Gorshkov has recently said:

*. . . the disruption of the ocean line of communications, the special arteries feeding the*

Soviet Naval Infantry practice beach assault disembarking from their amphibious BTR-60 armored personnel carriers.

*military and economic potentials of those (the enemy) countries, has continued to be one of the most important of the Navy's missions.*

## Support Of Ground Forces

The Soviet Union's geographical position and its consequent status as primarily a land power demand that the Soviet Navy protect the seaward flanks of the army. Although the Soviet Navy has been recast into an ocean-going force with major offensive as well as defensive tasks, support of the ground forces still remains an important mission. This task, of course, entails protecting the army's seaward flanks from attack by enemy naval and amphibious forces, providing naval gunfire and logistics support and carrying out amphibious assaults in support of land operations. The operations involved would appear to be most likely in the Baltic and Black Seas as spearheads to obtain control of the Danish and Turkish Straits, respectively, and also in assaults against Northern Norway and possibly the Japanese Straits.

The Soviets maintain several SVERDLOV class cruisers, with 12 six-inch guns, and a large short-range assault force of amphibious ships and naval infantry ("marines"), presumably to conduct flanking operations and to seize key coastal areas in support of ground operations. Soviet military doctrine calls for the small naval infantry force, augmented at the initial assault, to be followed by army units which are trained in amphibious operations. Several army divisions periodically practice amphibious landings, and a large and readily adaptable merchant fleet is available to supplement the amphibious ships in supporting these movements. Airborne operations are often conducted in conjunction with amphibious exercises. Also, the diesel and nuclear powered submarines armed with short range ballistic missiles apparently have theater strike roles in support of ground operations. In 1976 six GOLF II class SSBs, each with three 700-nautical mile nuclear ballistic missiles, were the first submarines to be assigned to the Baltic Fleet in this role.

## Support of State Policy

The Soviet leadership in the last two decades has awakened to the value of a powerful navy and other

11

elements of sea power as tangible support for their nation's foreign economic, political and military policies. The Soviets have discovered the tenets which Alfred Thayer Mahan postulated in his book *The Influence of Sea Power Upon History* (1890), and what some of the tsars before them realized: a navy is well suited for an active and useful role as an instrument of state policy in peacetime as well as in wartime.

Because of its great operational flexibility, its visibility and the lack of political restraints on the movement of warships on the high seas, a fleet is able to demonstrate power in distant areas to support national objectives. Of all the armed services, a navy is best suited for this world-wide role because it is not restricted by the sovereignty of airspace over land or by territorial rights.

The tutor to the Kremlin in naval matters, Admiral Gorshkov, has stated:

*Warships appearing directly off the shore represent a real threat of operations whose time and execution are determined by those in command. Whereas such a threat was quite great in the past, today it is much more so, since modern warships are platforms for nuclear-missile weaponry and aircraft whose range can cover the entire territory of a state.*

The Soviet Navy maintains a fleet in the Mediterranean on a continuous basis. Seen here at the southern entrance to the Aegean Sea are, clockwise from top, a KASHIN missile destroyer, a VYTEGRALES class cargo ship, a KASHIN with a NANUCHKA missile ship astern, and a KOTLIN destroyer with a NANUCHKA astern.

He has also written:

*Navies . . . are constantly being utilized as an instrument of state policy in peacetime. In this regard, navies have assumed particular significance under today's conditions. The mobility of the fleet and its flexibility in the event limited military conflicts are brewing, permit it to have an influence on coastal countries, to employ and extend a military threat to any level, beginning with a show of military strength and ending with the landing of forces ashore.*

Taking Admiral Gorshkov at his word, one can observe that "support of state policy" goes beyond the peacetime "showing the flag" role. In recent years the Soviets have not been timid in using their Navy to support client states and friends in time of crisis. Prime examples are the 1967 and 1973 Arab-Israeli Wars, the Bangledesh War of 1971, the Cuban intervention in the Angolan civil war during 1975, the Ethiopian civil war of 1978, the Sino-Vietnam conflict of 1978 and the recent invasion of Afghanistan.

Today, Soviet naval forces are deployed continuously on several seas and perform a variety of political and military tasks. They demonstrate Soviet military might during port visits, assert Soviet rights on the high seas, protect the interests of Soviet merchant and fishing fleets, demonstrate support for Soviet clients and inhibit Western military initiatives: The Russian bear has grown webbed feet.

## E. The Future

The Soviet Navy can be expected to seek to expand its capabilities in various functional areas in the years to come. The Soviets might seek to expand their now limited ability to extend conventional power ashore to areas distant from the Soviet Union into a full-fledged seaborne projection capability with its attendant sea control, amphibious assault and sea-based aviation forces. This possibility is discussed further in Section 4.

As the Soviet Union expands its world trade and becomes increasingly dependent on foreign commodities and imported technology, it will find it necessary to provide protection to its distant sea lines of communications.

Another emerging mission for the Soviet Navy, as well as the other navies of the world, will be the protection of facilities exploiting ocean economic resources. With or without the introduction of a new International Law of the Sea Treaty, exploitation of the seabed and fishing resources will become an increasingly important issue among the world's nations.

# Section 3. The Soviet Navy Today

*Our country has built a modern Navy and sent it out into the ocean in order to support our own state interests and to reliably defend us from attack from the vast ocean sector.*

*Admiral of the Fleet of the Soviet Union*
*S.G. GORSHKOV*

The Soviet Navy has dramatically increased at sea operations since the early 1960s with particular emphasis in political-economic crisis areas such as the eastern Mediterranean and Indian Ocean. Along with this quantitative increase there has been an increase in warship capabilities. At the same time, U.S. naval forces and operations have declined considerably.

## A. Operations

Today the Soviet Navy maintains ships at sea in a number of areas of the world far distant from the U.S.S.R. Descriptions of these ships, their weapons and their crews are found in subsequent sections of this publication.

Long range deployments have increased dramatically since the early 1960s. Until then, Soviet ships remained primarily in coastal areas, adjacent to their major fleet operating bases in the Baltic Sea, Arctic Ocean and Northwest Pacific Ocean. After Admiral Gorshkov's "go to sea" order of 1963, a dramatic increase in Soviet operations outside of coastal areas began. Figure 2 shows this trend, with U.S. Navy ship deployments provided for comparison. U.S. operations decreased dramatically in the early 1970s, partially as a result of the reduction of our active fleet by almost one-half of its peak strength during the Vietnam War (1967–1968).

### Submarines

From the 1960s onward there has been a marked increase in submarine activity involving torpedo and cruise missile attack submarines and strategic missile submarines. The latter has particular significance because of the greatly reduced flight time of 8 to 12 minutes of the SS-N-6 SLBM compared to the 20 to 30-minute flight time of intercontinental ballistic missiles (ICBMs) launched from the Soviet Union, or the several-hour flight time of manned bombers from the Soviet Union to attack targets in the United States. The Soviet SLBM capability could threaten U.S. bomber bases as well as national command centers, possibly destroying bombers and "pinning down" missiles before they could be launched. (SLBMs currently are considered to lack the accuracy to destroy Minuteman ICBMs in hardened underground silos.)

The earliest Soviet strategic-missile submarines, constructed in the late 1950s, posed little threat to the continental United States. These submarines had limited underwater endurance, could only fire missiles while on the surface, and were armed with only two or three SARK (SS-N-4) missiles which had a range of about 350 nautical miles and poor accuracy. (Many of these earlier SSBs and SSBNs were later equipped with 700 NM range SS-N-5 missiles). These submarines apparently had major problems. One GOLF class was lost in the North Pacific in 1968 and one HOTEL class SSBN experienced serious engine trouble in the North Atlantic early in 1972. (The HOTEL was towed back to the Soviet Union on the surface.)

The Soviet SLBM situation changed radically in 1967 when they sent their first YANKEE class submarine to sea. This nuclear powered submarine, armed with 16 SS-N-6 missiles having an initial range of 1,300 nautical miles and capable of submerged launch, was more difficult to detect and had a potent strike capability. During 1968, YANKEE class SSBNs began patrols in the Atlantic, periodically coming within range of U.S. cities. In 1971, YANKEE SSBN patrols began off the Pacific coast. The later DELTA class SSBNs, with a missile range in excess of 4,000 nautical miles, are within

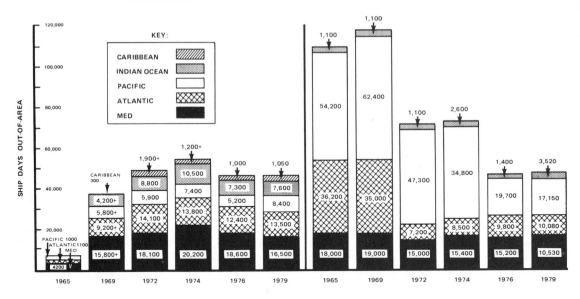

**Figure 2**
Trends in U.S. — Soviet Naval Operations
Ship Days Out — of — Area

striking distance of New York City or Washington, D.C. while still in well protected Soviet home port areas on the Arctic coast. This same situation applies in the Pacific, where DELTA class SSBNs at their base of Petropavlovsk on the Siberian coast are within missile range of western U.S. cities such as Seattle and San Francisco.

Whereas just over a decade ago the Soviets had a relatively small strategic submarine force with a few short-range missiles, today's Soviet SLBMs provide a significant and increasing percentage of Soviet strategic nuclear strike capability.

The massive SSBN effort, which has produced 66 nuclear powered submarines in ten years, has not detracted from the Soviet attack submarine programs. Several classes of nuclear and diesel submarines armed with torpedos and guided missiles are also under construction. These general purpose submarines now roam the world's oceans in support of Kremlin policies, ready to challenge an adversary's control of the sea.

The modernization of the Soviet submarine force, despite a slow reduction of overall numbers of submarines, has resulted in significant increases in submarine operations in many areas of the world compared to 20 years ago. More importantly, the

capabilities of the Soviet submarine force increase steadily as new nuclear powered boats join the fleet at the rate of about eight per year.

### Mediterranean

The most significant Soviet deployments have been in the crisis-plagued Eastern Mediterranean. Soviet out-of-area ship days in the Mediterranean increased from approximately 4,000 in 1965 to more than 16,500 in 1979. An out-of-area ship day is defined as one in which a navy ship is deployed beyond the normal operating and training areas of home waters. Thus, 16,500 ship days means an average of about 45 ships in the area every day of the year. In the early 1970s the Soviets apparently achieved the general levels of deployments they perceived as adequate for "support of state interest" purposes. Usually, 10 to 15 percent of the Soviet ocean going fleet is operating "out-of-area." The Kremlin leadership, however, has been quick to increase the number of deployed ships to areas of crisis or elsewhere for other perceived needs.

The Soviet Mediterranean fleet normally consists of:

8 to 10 torpedo attack submarines

2 to 3 cruise missile attack submarines

2 to 4 cruisers, some or all armed with guided missiles, and periodically, aviation ships of the MOSKVA or KIEV classes

9 to 12 destroyers and patrol ships, some armed with guided missiles

1 to 3 minesweepers

1 to 3 amphibious ships

15 to 20 auxiliary ships

5 to 6 survey, oceanographic research, and intelligence collection ships

The presence of these ships increases Soviet political and military options in the Mediterranean. For example, shortly after the June 1967 Arab-Israeli war began, the Soviets sent ships to the Egyptian harbors of Port Said and Alexandria in an obvious move to deter Israeli attacks against those ports.

The air bases in Egypt, used by the Soviets from 1967 until 1972, permitted Soviet land-based naval reconnaissance and ASW aircraft to operate over the eastern Mediterranean without overflying Greece or Turkey. The loss of Egyptian air bases to the Soviets in 1972 unquestionably reduced Soviet military capabilities in the eastern Mediterranean. However, the Soviet naval position in 1972 after loss of the air bases was still far superior to that of a decade earlier.

In addition to the large number of fighter aircraft provided by the Soviets to Middle Eastern countries, BLINDER supersonic bombers have also been delivered to Iraq and Libya.

A large number of missile-armed patrol boats have been delivered by the Soviets to Third World countries in the Mediterranean, as well as diesel torpedo-attack submarines of the FOXTROT class to Libya and WHISKEY and ROMEO classes to Egypt.

The Soviets continue to press for base facilities on the Mediterranean littoral. Besides limited base

**The BEAR D reconnaissance aircraft provides the Soviet Navy with long-range reconnaissance and missile guidance. Note the counter-rotating propellers on the BEAR's four turboprop engines, the "chin" radome, and nose refueling probe. A PHANTOM of Fighter Squadron 41 is the "escort."**

support facilities in use in Tartus, Syria, the Soviet Navy, on a contract basis, utilizes overhaul and repair facilities at shipyards in Yugoslavia, Tunisia and Greece. The naval leadership no doubt desires more permanent arrangements for bases with greater facilities than presently available to them. A prime candidate from the Soviet point of view must be the old French naval base of Mers-el-Kabir in Algeria.

The Soviet Mediterranean Squadron (SOVMED-RON) is maintained and supplied primarily at anchorages in international waters. Although this routine is adequate in peacetime, under wartime conditions such a logistics operation would be most vulnerable.

Although their Navy operates in the Mediterranean under a number of restrictive conditions, the Soviets are constantly striving to eliminate or minimize those restrictions. Access to the gates of the Mediterranean is controlled by powers outside the Soviet sphere of influence: the Suez Canal is controlled by Egypt; the Atlantic egress by Spain and the British bastion at Gibraltar; and the Turkish Straits to the Black Sea by Turkey, a member of NATO. The Turkish Straits are also regulated by an international treaty, the Montreux Convention, which the Soviets probably perceive more as a blessing than a curse. Although Soviet warships must give advance notice and are restricted in the numbers which may pass through per day, navies of countries not washed by Black Sea waters have much greater restrictions placed upon their warships operating in that sea.

From all appearances the Soviets look upon the eastern Mediterranean as *"Mare Nostrum,"* and consider those waters critical to their national defense. Because of this they will no doubt continue to

The aircraft carrier KIEV—originally called an antisubmarine cruiser by the Soviets—adds a new dimension to Soviet naval capabilities. The "flattop," displacing about 37,000 tons, has the potential for antisubmarine, fleet air defense, reconnaissance, and antiship strike and close air support operations. Note the gun, missile, and rocket armament on her bow and the angled flight deck.

strive for port access and base facilities as well as overflight rights as they work to extend their political influence in the Mediterranean area. They will undoubtedly continue in their attempts to weaken NATO's southern flank by driving a wedge between the West and the vital Mid-east by flexing naval muscle in this historic cross roads of civilizations and cultures—the Mediterranean Sea.

## Caribbean

Soviet naval deployments to the Caribbean began in mid-1969 when a task force consisting of a missile-armed cruiser, two missile-armed destroyers, three attack submarines (one nuclear powered) and three auxiliary ships operated in the Caribbean, making port visits to Cuba.

One year later, another Soviet task force operated in the Caribbean and still others have subsequently steamed in those waters. On past occasions, nuclear powered cruise missile submarines and conventionally powered GOLF class ballistic missile submarines have operated in Cuban waters. On a number of occasions these ships have operated in the Gulf of Mexico off the Louisiana and Texas coasts. Besides showing the flag in the Caribbean, these Soviet warships have participated often in training exercises with Cuban naval units. Through 1979, there had been 20 naval deployments to Cuba, in addition to the stationing of a fleet tug there and regular replenishment visits by intelligence collectors and survey ships. In this regard, the Soviets have shown a varying interest in the naval base at Cienfuegos on the south coast of Cuba. The Cuban Navy is now provided almost entirely with Soviet equipment, including two FOXTROT class submarines.

In April of 1970, a pair of long-range BEAR D naval reconnaissance aircraft flew non-stop from bases in the Murmansk area on Russia's Arctic coast, down the Norwegian Sea, across the Atlantic, and landed in Cuba. Other reconnaissance aircraft have followed in what have become nearly routine flights, with some of these aircraft subsequently flying reconnaissance missions off the U.S. Altantic coast. (One of these aircraft was accidently lost off Newfoundland in November 1975.) Because the Soviets can no longer use airfields in Guinea, West Africa, BEAR D deployments to or from Angola now stage through Cuba. By the end of 1979, there had been a total of 50 BEAR D deployments to Cuba; BEAR D aircraft usually deploy in pairs.

The periodic presence of U.S.S.R. naval ships in the Caribbean demonstrates Soviet support for the Castro government. This presence could inhibit

U.S. options in the area inasmuch as their presence inplies support for intervention or revolution in Central American nations.

## Atlantic

Over the past two decades the Soviet Navy has regularly exercised in the Norwegian Sea. Their major efforts are concentrated in the spring in contrast to annual NATO naval exercises, usually held in the fall. Most Soviet exercise activity has taken place north of the Greenland-Iceland-United Kingdom (GIUK) gap. In recent years, however, Soviet submarines, surface warships, and aircraft have operated more frequently further south in the Western Approaches to Europe. This is in addition to those units transiting the area for the Mediterranean or Cuba or to the open ocean for ballistic missile patrols.

Besides the aforementioned activity, the Soviets regularly maintain intelligence collection ships (AGI) on patrol off the Western SSBN bases in Scotland, the United States and until its disestablishment in 1979, the base at Rota, Spain.

In the South Atlantic, Soviet warships have maintained a nearly continuous patrol off the African west coast since late 1970. The appearance of these ships in the Gulf of Guinea "coincided" with the release by the Accra government of two Soviet fishing craft impounded some months earlier. Further, Soviet warships appeared in the aftermath of a Portugese-supported raid against Conakry, Guinea in November 1970, possible in an effort to deter further attacks.

Starting in the Spring of 1973, pairs of naval BEAR D reconnaissance aircraft made periodic deployments to Conakry, Guinea, from the Soviet Arctic to fly surveillance missions against U.S. Navy ships in the Central Atlantic.

During the Angolan civil war in 1975–1976, Soviet warships were dispatched to patrol the waters near Angola as an encouragement for the Soviet backed Cuban intervention in support of one of the rebel groups. Simultaneously, Soviet aircraft flew in Cuban troops and supplies while the Soviet merchant marines mounted a massive sealift of war material. Since that time, BEAR D reconnaissance aircraft have occasionally operated out of Luanda, Angola, which allows this aircraft coverage of most of the South Atlantic.

Aside from the small South African Navy, the Soviet West African squadron is the only continuous naval presence in that area of the South Atlantic, astride the vital oil route from the Persian Gulf to

Western Europe.

## Indian Ocean

Soviet ships regularly operate in the Indian Ocean, generally with a missile-armed cruiser, several destroyers, an amphibious ship, a submarine and a number of support ships. (The Soviet squadron averaged about 20 ships until the crisis of 1979-80 when the average was about 30.) These ships demonstrate support of Soviet interests on the coasts of the three continents washed by the Indian Ocean. This regular deployment, which commenced in 1968, has been the key element in Soviet relations with India and several of the newer countries in the area.

The Soviets' need for port access and base facilities in the Indian Ocean is even greater than that in the Mediterranean Sea. A glance at a globe will show the great transit distance from Soviet Pacific and Black Sea bases (particularly if the Suez Canal is closed) to the Indian Ocean. A look at the southern border of the U.S.S.R. in the Trans-Caucasus area reveals what drives the historical Russian desire to gain direct access to the Indian Ocean, which no doubt contributed to the Soviet decision to invade Afghanistan in late 1979.

During the 1970s, the Soviets built several naval and air facilities in Somalia in a strategic position to control the Red Sea and access to the Suez Canal. In 1977, after a falling-out with the regime in Somalia, the Soviets were forced out of their bases there. They subsequently resorted to the use of facilities in Aden, South Yemen, and Ethiopia, to support their Indian Ocean Squadron (SOVINDRON). MAY maritime patrol aircraft, operating from Aden, have frequently tracked U.S. naval units in the Arabian Sea. During the recent buildup of forces as a result of the Iran and Afghan crises, the Soviets operated as many as six MAYs from Aden and Ethiopia.

The Soviet Indian Ocean squadron also has used port facilities in Iraq in the past, and regularly makes calls to selected ports on the Indian Ocean littoral. Soviet naval ships visit ports in Mozambique, the Seychelles Islands, Mauritius, India, and Sri Lanka.

The Soviets have shown a willingness to expand their naval commitment in the Indian Ocean whenever they believe their interests to be threatened. During the Indian-Pakistan War of 1971; immediately after the Arab-Israeli War of 1973; in support of Ethiopian-Somalia conflict; during the Iranian revolution in early 1979 and the Iranian hostage crisis; and the Afghanistan invasion in late 1979, the Soviets increased the number of warships deployed to the Indian Ocean including cruise missile submarines. This served to counter U.S. carrier forces, which had been sent from the Pacific and Atlantic Fleets as well as to support their "clients."

In the aftermath of the Arab-Israeli and Indian-Pakistan wars the Soviet Navy provided harbor clearance and minesweeping services to both Bangledesh and Egypt, respectively. They helped in clearing the port of Chittagong and the southern approaches to the Suez Canal. One of the ships involved in the Suez operation was the aviation cruiser LENINGRAD.

Although the Suez Canal is now open, making the area "east of Suez" more accessible to the Soviet Black Sea Fleet, the majority of Soviet ships which deploy to the Indian Ocean make the long trip from the Pacific Ocean Fleet. It is on long transits such as these that the Soviets often tow submarines and smaller combatants as one way of reducing "wear and tear" on these ships, extending the time between engine overhauls and conserving fuel.

With the termination of extensive Bangledesh and Egyptian operations in 1974 the number of Soviet naval ships and, therefore, the total number of "ship days" in the Indian Ocean dropped to "normal" numbers. The Soviets now average a force of about 20 ships in the Indian Ocean, the majority of which are naval auxiliaries. In comparison, the U.S. Navy's standing commitment to the Indian Ocean area consists of one amphibious ship converted to a flagship and two or three destroyers or frigates.

U.S. carrier task forces have deployed periodically to the Indian Ocean, but only with considerable difficulty in ship scheduling and logistics. Since late 1979, with the Iran crisis and the invasion of Afghanistan by the Soviets, both the U.S. and Soviet naval commitments in the Indian Ocean have, nonetheless, expanded significantly.

## Pacific Ocean

In the Pacific, the Soviets initiated long range surface ship operations during the 1950s when relations between Moscow and Peking were amiable. Subsequently, aid to Indonesia and other Soviet interests in the Pacific basin led to expanded Soviet naval operations.

During the fall of 1971 a Soviet force consisting of a guided-missile cruiser, two missile-armed destroyers, three submarines and a tanker crossed the Pacific to the Gulf of Alaska, and then turned south to steam within 25 miles of Diamond Head,

Hawaii, before returning to Soviet Pacific coast ports. Soviet Pacific Ocean Fleet ships were used to collect intelligence and as an occasional show of force against U.S. Seventh Fleet during the Vietnam War. Soviet warships periodically visit many parts of the Pacific where, until a decade ago, Soviet military power was discussed but never seen. As an example, two Soviet missile destroyers and an oiler made a port visit to Vancouver, Canada in 1976.

Soviet AGIs are regularly deployed off Guam to monitor the arrivals and departures of U.S. ballistic missile submarines operating from there. AGIs also operate off the U.S. West Coast with some regularity. A number of Soviet space support and recovery ships deploy to the North Central Pacific, an area into which the Soviets test fire their long-range ballistic missiles.

Recently the Soviet Navy has been using port facilities and airfields in Vietnam to support expanded deployments in the South China Sea. Soviet naval presence increased in this area during the Sino-Vietnam War of 1979. This increased presence has been maintained and includes the regular deployment of BEAR D and F aircraft.

## B. Trends

An analysis of the Soviet Navy during the past two decades reveals (1) significant diversity and im-provement in warship, aircraft, and weapons capabilities; (2) large increases in at-sea and distant deployment operations; (3) commitments by the Soviets to strive for a Navy "second to none;" and (4) increased awareness by the Soviet leadership of the leverage which accures to a nation with sizeable and strong maritime resources, especially a large, modern navy.

Several comparisons of trends related to the U.S. and Soviet navies support these observations.

The Soviet Navy is by far the largest in the world today in terms of numbers of ships, primarily because of the large numbers of submarines, small combatants, mine warfare ships, and auxilaries in its inventory. While the preceding is an important point, estimating the relative capabilities of navies is not just a matter of comparing force levels, or matching distant deployments and exercises. All of these are factors in estimating the naval balance, but just as important are weapons, sensors, communications, and personnel, as well as trends in doctrine, development, procurement, and national will and commitment. In assessing the relative merits of navies, the prime point is which navy can best accomplish its mission under the real or potential threat of its adversaries.

Although the total numerical inventory is slowly declining, for the foreseeable future the Soviet Navy is expected to continue to have the world's largest number of warships.

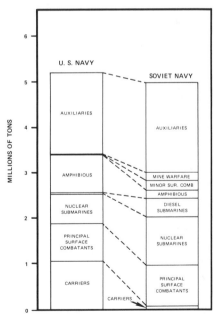

FIGURE 3
NUMBER OF ACTIVE SHIPS 1979

FIGURE 4
FULL LOAD DISPLACEMENT OF SHIPS IN COMMISSION 1979

It cannot be ignored that as a result of the Soviet leadership's determined policy to expand all facets of the sea power equation, the Soviet Navy is continuing to expand its recently acquired "blue water" capabilities. Indications are those efforts will not diminish over the next few years.

Figures 3 and 4 depict the comparisons of the numbers and tonnages between the various ship categories in the Soviet Navy and the U.S. Navy. It should be noted that the U.S. Navy greatly exceeds the Soviet Fleet in aircraft carriers; and although the Soviet Navy has more amphibious ships, the U.S. Navy amphibious lift capability is much greater. Figure 4 demonstrates that if one subtracts the U.S. Navy's 13 aircraft carriers, the Soviet Navy has a greater tonnage. Thus, the U.S. Navy's tonnage advantage and most capable conventional strike capabilities are in a fewer number of ships. However, the Soviets have numerical and tonnage leadership in several important categories.

### Surface Combatant

The number of Soviet principal surface combatants (frigates and larger) is greater than that of the U.S. Navy, although more than 100 of the Soviet ships are frigates which are significantly smaller than their U.S. counterparts.

The principal surface combatants which the Soviets are building today have greater range, firepower, and electronics capabilities than in the past.

The modern ships of the Soviet Navy are among the fastest and most heavily armed in the world. They are of innovative modern design, graceful yet purposeful in appearance, and have contributed greatly to elevating the prestige and power of the Soviet Union among the world's nations.

Present building programs include about 12 hulls under construction in four new classes of large warships (including a 22,000-ton nuclear powered cruiser) and the continued construction of KIEV class carriers and several frigate classes.

The Soviet Navy has led the world in the use of cruise-missiles in naval warfare. Since the installation of the SS-N-1 cruise missile on the KILDEN and KRUPNYY classes of destroyers in the late 1950s, the Soviets have extensively developed and deployed this type of weapon. Today the Soviet Navy has over 20 cruisers, carriers, and destroyers; about 65 submarines; and 300 land-based aircraft armed with antiship cruise missiles. The first major U.S. weapon of this type, the HARPOON, entered service in 1977 (nearly 20 years after introduction of missiles to the Soviet Navy). The U.S. Navy had not emphasized the development of the cruise missile as an antiship weapon because of greater capabilities inherent in carrier aircraft. However, as the number of our aircraft carriers was reduced, the development of the HARPOON and TOMAHAWK cruise missiles was undertaken by the U.S. Navy. An ambitious HARPOON installation plan for aircraft, submarines and surface combatants will greatly

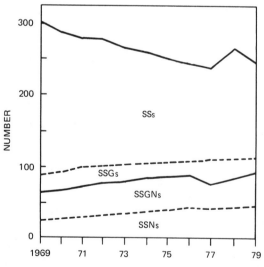

Figure 5. SOVIET GENERAL PURPOSE SUBMARINES

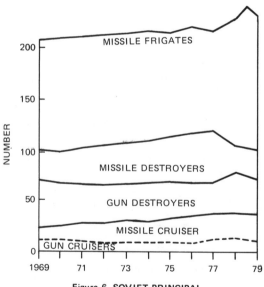

Figure 6. SOVIET PRINCIPAL SURFACE COMBATANTS

The underway replenishment ship BORIS CHILIKIN refuels the helicopter carrier MOSKVA at sea. After long relying primarily on their merchant marine for overseas support of naval forces, the Soviets are building a large force of modern UNREP ships.

reduce the Soviet cruise missile advantage. Although the U.S. Navy may close the gap in numbers of cruise missile systems and sophistication of guidance systems, the Soviets will, in some of their systems, retain an advantage in range and warhead size.

Critics often tend to write off the threat from the Soviet's smaller combatants (those less than 1,000 tons). For the most part they operate close to the Soviet coasts; however, the Soviets continue to pay attention to their coastal forces for obvious reasons. The Soviet Union is surrounded by a number of strong coastal navies which are viewed as threats. This situation exists to varying degrees in all four fleet areas, but it is greatest in the Baltic. Thus, the Soviets maintain the world's largest small combatant force (many units of which are missile armed) and the largest mine warfare force as a means of controlling their coastal seas. Periodically these coastal forces operate in the regional sea such as the Norwegian and Mediterranean, where they can directly threaten U.S. naval forces.

The Soviets have developed several new types of small combatants with emphasis on hydrofoil design, missile armament and gas-turbine power.

## Submarines

The Soviets have led the world in production of submarines in the post-World War II period. Since the end of the war, Soviet shipyards have built over 600 submarines (compared to about 140 for the United States). Of particular significance has been the Soviet emphasis on nuclear-power submarines. The Soviet Union has completed more and larger nuclear powered submarines than the United States.

The Soviet Union maintains a large submarine construction capacity which they have expanded significantly in the past decade. Submarine production is currently being used at less than 50 percent of its estimated capacity. Submarines are produced in five building yards in the U.S.S.R., while presently only two U.S. yards are constructing submarines. The hugh shipbuilding complex at Severodvinsk on the White Sea may well have a greater nuclear submarine building capacity than that of the United States, Great Britain and France combined.

Over the last several years the Soviets have built about 10 new submarines a year, most of them nuclear powered. By contrast, the U.S. has built an average of three nuclear powered submarines per year. It is anticipated that the Soviets will continue to build submarines at near the present rate. New units of the TYPHOON, OSCAR, ALFA, VICTOR and TANGO classes will probably be included in this future production.

The Soviets have built diesel and nuclear powered submarines which can launch cruise missiles. The U.S. Navy is just beginning to deploy the HARPOON missile in submarines, and is developing a submarine-launched TOMAHAWK. The Soviets have also developed a weapon similar to the U.S. Navy's SUBROC, an underwater-launched missile which flies a relatively short distance and carries an antisubmarine torpedo or nuclear depth charge.

The Soviet Navy continues to build diesel submarines to fill what Admiral Gorshkov says is a continuing need, both the TANGO class, a modern attack submarine for fleet use, and the ubiquitous FOXTROT class, the latter for foreign sales. Diesel

powered auxiliary submarines are also being built probably for rescue and research work.

The Soviet submarine force remains as the dominant branch of the Soviet Navy. Although the total number of submarines has been slowly decreasing as older diesel craft are retired, the numbers of nuclear powered and missile-armed submarines continues to increase. In comparison with U.S. submarines, it is estimated the Soviets still lag in antisubmarine sensor and weapon capabilities as well as submarine quieting techniques.

## Aviation

Soviet Naval Aviation has taken two significant steps in the last several years: the introduction of a sea-based, fixed-wing capability on the aircraft carrier KIEV and the introduction of the swing-wing, supersonic, missile-armed BACKFIRE bomber.

The Vertical Take-Off and Landing (VTOL) FOR-

The Soviet Navy is increasing its capability for underway replenishment at sea. The BEREZINA, a replenishment oiler and one of the largest ships in the Soviet Navy, refuels simultaneously the carrier KIEV, a KRESTA II class cruiser and a MOD KASHIN class destroyer.

GER aircraft can operate from the KIEV class carriers. Although of limited capabilities, the FORGER nevertheless gives a new dimension to the Soviet Navy. It is the embryo of what the Soviets have always lacked, the ability to provide air cover and air striking power as an indigenous part of a fleet operating in distant waters.

Soviet naval leaders stopped "bad-mouthing" aircraft carriers a number of years ago and now openly advocate carriers larger than the KIEV class. There is considerable evidence that the Soviets will introduce a larger carrier class sometime in the late 1980s. It appears logical that such a large carrier would probably be nuclear powered and operate conventional takeoff and landing (CTOL) aircraft.

It is significant that supersonic BACKFIRE bombers are being supplied to the Navy in about the same numbers as they are to the Soviet Air Forces' Long Range Aviation. The antiship mission of Soviet Naval Aviation remains a high priority.

The airborne ASW components of the Soviet Navy consist of HORMONE, HAZE, and HOUND helicopters, and MAIL, MAY and BEAR F fixed-wing aircraft. Over the last decade the Soviets have undertaken considerable research and development on ekronoplanes or "Wing-In-Ground" (WIG) effect vehicles. Some of this effort has been directed toward naval applications. Speculation is that the Soviets could be developing an antisubmarine or transport type WIG.

## Soviet Exercises

Coupled with the increase in ship numbers and capabilities, there has been a related increase in at-sea operations, as discussed previously. As Soviet warships have gone farther from their home ports and spent more time on the high seas, they have also increased the complexity of their naval exercises. To date the largest of these were two OKEAN (Russian for ocean) exercises conducted in the spring of 1970 and again in 1975.

These were the two largest Soviet peacetime naval exercises in history, with warships simultaneously conducting maneuvers in Atlantic, Mediterranean, Indian, and Pacific Ocean areas. Over 200 submarines, surface combatants, and support ships participated in OKEAN 70, and about 120 ships in OKEAN 75. The maneuvers included antisubmarine, anti-carrier, sea lines interdiction, convoy escort and amphibious landing operations. Land-based naval aircraft, as well as planes from the Soviet Air Defense Forces and Long-Range Aviation, participated in the maneuvers.

The electronics-laden island structure of the KIEV helps to demonstrate the allocation of technological resources by the Soviet Union to the development of a modern and highly capable fleet.

It appeared that these exercises were coordinated from Soviet Naval Headquarters in Moscow. From Soviet writings it is evident that a major aim of the exercises was to test the Soviet ocean surveillance system and the overall command, control, and communications ($C^3$) systems in world-wide scenarios. These two large exercises clearly demonstrated the scope and range of Soviet naval capabilities.

The Soviet Navy exercises routinely in antisubmarine, anticarrier, and amphibious warfare in home operating waters and when on distant deployments. For example, in the spring of 1977 the Northern and Baltic Fleets jointly conducted a large-scale exercise in the Norwegian, Barents and Baltic Seas. Also, the Soviets conducted ASW exercises in the Gulf of Mexico with Cuban forces and combined missile attack and amphibious exercises in the Baltic with the East German and Polish navies.

In a report to Congress in 1979, the U.S. Navy's Director of Naval Intelligence, Rear Admiral Sumner Shapiro, summed up the trends we expect in the future Soviet Navy as follows:

> *Continuing construction of larger, more versatile ships with increased capabilities. Replacement of older ships with modern missile warships with increased emphasis on electronics. SSBN force improvement through acquisition of longer ranged, more sophisticated weapons. Increased capability of general purpose submarine forces to operate in open ocean areas. Improvements in sea-based aviation (VTOL and helicopters) capabilities for antisubmarine, antisurface, and antiair warfare from seaborne platforms.*
>
> *Replacement of land-based older bomber aircraft with newer, more sophisticated, cruise missile-equipped BACKFIRE aircraft.*
>
> *The continuing improvement in amphibious assault lift capability.*

## C. Limitations

As has already been noted, the Soviet Navy is not "ten feet" tall. The third edition of this book noted the Soviets were "five feet ten inches and growing," probably they should be characterized today as "six feet tall and growing." But the Soviet Navy does have significant problems because of its limitations. It must be noted that over the years the trends show the Soviets attempting to alleviate their problems where they can by overcoming or minimizing their limitations. It is this trend that must concern the West, for as the Soviets expand their naval options and capabilities, the Western navies' options are reduced.

Rear Admiral Shapiro, during his congressional report, also noted several Soviet naval weaknesses. Included is a limited capability to conduct open ocean ASW and underway replenishment capability; inadequate sea-based tactical air forces; and geographical constraints which inhibit access to the open ocean.

The Soviets are seeking to improve their open-ocean ASW capability by a variety of methods. This includes extensive efforts in basic research and development in several detection fields, and a sizeable allocation of resources to ASW weapons procurement. Most modern Soviet surface combatants, a significant segment of the submarines force, and many of the combat aircraft of their navy are dedicated primarily to hunting Western submarines. Fortunately, their capability to find them does not appear to be improving much.

Sea-based air power will increase significantly in the next few years as additional KIEV class ships with their FORGER VTOL aircraft join the fleet augmented by more BACKFIRE strike aircraft. The current lack of shipboard fighter aircraft is partially offset by the extensive use of medium and short-range surface-to-air missiles and a variety of guns for close-in defense against aircraft and missiles.

The defensive limitations of Soviet strike and reconnaissance aircraft can be mitigated somewhat by overseas basing, such as has been done periodically by Soviet naval aircraft flying from Cuba, Vietnam, Guinea, Iraq, Angola, Somalia and, until 1972, Egypt. Of course, as the Soviet Navy deploys more fighter aircraft to sea, the successful defense of formations of naval strike aircraft is more likely. Lastly, the BACKFIRE bomber has supersonic dash speed, greater range, and better low-altitude performance than its predecessor, the BADGER.

The Soviet Navy has no insurmountable problems replenishing and maintaining its distant deployed fleets during peacetime in that the Soviet Navy employs tenders and oilers in anchorages in international waters as its prime means of logistic support. Many of the oilers operate under the flag of the Soviet Merchant Marine. Although the Soviets have improved their alongside underway replenishment of liquids in recent years, their ability to transfer ammunition and other solids in the same manner is still lacking.

Additionally, shore-based logistic and repair facilities are used to varying degrees in foreign ports where the Soviets have managed to gain some degree of access. Countries which provide such facilities include Syria, Cuba, Yugoslavia, Tunisia, Guinea, Angola, South Yemen, Greece, Singapore, Ethiopia and Vietnam.

During a war such port facilities might be denied or become inaccessible, and the anchorages would be vulnerable. The underway replenishment of fuels, ammunition, consumables, and repair parts would then be required to sustain warships at great distances from their home ports in prolonged periods of conflict. The Soviet Navy has been slow in developing underway replenishment capabilities and techniques; it has almost exclusively concentrated on refueling. The movement of solid stores between ships underway, and helicopter delivery techniques, have not been practiced to a great extent although the Soviets are quite adept at these movements in anchorages. During the last ten years the Soviets have introduced the BORIS CHILIKIN class of combination oiler-stores ship, and now have some six of these sophisticated underway replenishment ships in operation. Further, a number of Soviet naval and merchant oilers can provide alongside underway refueling as well as the slower astern method traditionally used by the Soviet Navy. Several smaller types of underway replenishment ships have been built for the Navy.

To meet the demands for a greater variety of fuels, ammunition, and provisions imposed by the introduction of aircraft carriers, the Soviets built a larger, multipurpose replenishment ship which carries two helicopters for vertical replenishment and is similar to the U.S. Navy's AOR design. This ship, the 40,000 ton BEREZINA, joined the fleet in 1978.

Through the centuries, Russia has been burdened with poor physical conformation of her coasts and geographic positions with respect to access to the open oceans. Today the Soviets have lessened some of these geographic limitations. For example, the scarcity of all-weather ports has been partially overcome with extensive use of icebreakers, and northern shipyards and bases have covered building ways and floating dry docks.

In the late 1950s, the significant ocean-going ships and submarines which the Soviets would use in the Atlantic were moved from the restricted waters of the Baltic to the Northern Fleet. Although the latter fleet had to contend with the rigorous Arctic climate, and had a much greater distance to travel to gain access to the North Atlantic, that access was a relatively open seaway not restricted by straits which could be easily controlled by the West. The Baltic Fleet today consists principally of a large number of smaller warships, diesel submarines, minesweepers, and amphibious ships. It is a fleet which, along with those of the East German and Polish Navies, is designed to control the Baltic and to provide support to the ground forces operating along the Baltic coasts. Under this arrangement the geographic constraint of the Danish Straits becomes less critical to the Soviets.

Similarly, the Black Sea Fleet's ability to go to sea through the NATO controlled Turkish Straits and Aegean Sea is a lesser problem because a num-

**Two MIRKA class small frigates close on a tanker and the missile cruiser-helicopter carrier MOSKVA in the Mediterranean. Some Soviet operational areas and missions are different than those of the U.S. Navy, hence many Soviet ships differ in design and size from their American contemporaries. The MIRKAs have combination diesel-gas turbine propulsion systems.**

ber of that fleet's ships normally are deployed in the Mediterranean. However, resupply from the Black Sea would be a problem in time of conflict.

The Soviet Pacific Ocean Fleet has been expanded in recent years and is now second only to the Northern Fleet in capabilities. To overcome the traditional restrictions on this fleet imposed by the Japanese Straits, the Soviets have developed a large naval complex at Petropavlovsk, on the sparsely populated Kamchatka Peninsula, which provides direct access to the Pacific Ocean. It is here that the bulk of the operational submarine force is based. But this area is at the end of a long and vulnerable supply line.

Lastly, it should be noted that where geographic conformation restricts Soviet access to the open oceans, these restrictions conversely assist the Soviets in defending those waters against Western maritime threats.

Another criticism leveled at the Soviet Navy is that it is a "one-shot" fleet, optimized for strong initial striking power with relatively limited offensive weapon reloads, namely, cruise missiles. This lack of endurance reflects Admiral Gorshkov's "battle of the first salvo" philosophy. This could be considered a limitation, but at the same time it permits the Soviet Navy to be optimized for a specific war situation. However, Soviet ships have a significant reload capability in torpedoes, guns, and surface-to-air missiles that is generally comparable to U.S. ships. Lastly, several of the new classes of warships and submarines have overcome this "shortcoming" by having an increased cruise missile load of 20 or more.

## D. Salesmanship

The statement has been made that the Soviets are achieving a political and psychological impact with their maritime forces far out of proportion to their size and potential. This is believed due to often exaggerated descriptions of Soviet naval power published in the West.

Not surprisingly, the same adjective-filled descriptions are trumpeted by the Soviet press and, probably of more significance, by the press of non-aligned or "third world" nations. In the same respect that "beauty is in the eye of the beholder," so is power in the eye of the beholder. In this situation the "beholder" is, to a large extent, the world that is using the seas more than ever before in history for political, resource, trade, and military purposes.

Soviet leaders—especially Admiral Gorshkov—unabashedly boast of the scope, range, influence, and power of Soviet naval forces. Admiral Gorshkov's recent book, *Sea Power of the State,* has been

widely distributed throughout the world as well as in the Soviet Union. Their navy is very much in the thoughts and words of the Soviet leadership. Whereas, as noted earlier, in the late 1950s Premier Nikita Khrushchev declared the obsolescence of big-ship surface fleets and cited cruisers as being useful only to carry admirals, the current Soviet leadership obviously has a different view of naval forces.

The regular visits of Soviet Party and State leaders as well as foreign officials to warships of the Soviet Navy demonstrate their endorsement of these ships and their operations. For example, commenting on the OKEAN exercise of 1970, the Soviet Minister of Defense at the time, the late Marshal of the Soviet Union A.A. Grechko, declared that the Navy "had grown up, strengthened, and is capable of reliably defending our state interests on the wide reaches of the world's oceans." And L.I. Brezhnev, the First Secretary of the Communist Part, has observed the reaction of the United States to Soviet naval efforts. He has explained the ability of the Soviet Navy to limit Western freedom of action by pointing to American reaction in this manner:

*The propaganda machine of the USA has launched a whole campaign concerning the Soviet Navy. Washington, you see, perceives a threat in the fact that our vessels appear in the Mediterranean, in the Indian Ocean, and in other seas. But at the same time their Sixth Fleet is constantly in the Mediterranean—at the side, as it were, of the Soviet Union, and the Seventh Fleet—off the shores of China and Indochina.*

As Soviet naval forces deploy farther on the high seas they also are visiting more foreign ports. Admiral Gorshkov stated in the early 1970s that in the previous three-year period:

*. . . some 1,000 combatants and auxiliary ships have visited the ports of 60 countries in Europe, Asia, Africa, and Latin America. More than 100,000 of our officers and rated and non-rated men have visited the shores of foreign states.*

What a contrast to 20 years or earlier when Soviet naval visits outside the Communist sphere did not average one per year.

As an indication that such an activity continues to increase, another Soviet admiral noted that in 1975 alone, the Navy had visited 82 ports in over 50 countries, and that some 80,000 Soviet officers and sailors had strolled on foreign shores.

Soviet sailors do not fill the local museums, restaurants, and bars as do American sailors, nor do they have significant funds. But, the Red sailors do go ashore, and their warships, modern and well kept, do ride at anchor in an increasing number of harbors. Their ships often carry bands and dance teams on these visits, and the local officials, and sometimes the public, are invited to tour the ships.

With this widespread, visible presence of the Soviet Navy in many areas of the world, and its threat of interposition as a shield to a client state or revolutionary movement (such as happened during the Angolan civil war and the Ethiopian-Somalia War), Western nations have had their peacetime political options greatly reduced. As French writer Michel Tatu observed:

*Landings of the type carried out by the United States in Lebanon in 1958 and in the Dominican Republic in 1965 would be more hazardous, if not entirely out of the question, today. On the other hand, a landing by Soviet "marines" to support some "progressive" regime or to help some minority faction in a power struggle is no longer inconceivable.*

As a means to achieve better understanding between the two superpower navies and their personnel, the U.S. Navy and Soviet Navy exchanged port visits in 1975. The United States sent a cruiser and destroyer to Leningrad and the Soviets sent two destroyers to Boston. Both visits were generously welcomed by their respective hosts, and large, enthusiastic crowds toured the visiting ships in both countries. Also, during the 1976 Operation Sail and International Naval Review of the United States' Bicentennial Independence Day Celebration, the largest sailing ship present was the beautiful square-rigged KRUZENSHTERN, a Soviet merchant marine

The Soviet merchant marine training bark KRUZENSHTERN was the largest participating ship in Operational Sail, a gathering of tall sailing ships during the American Bicentennial Celebration. The Soviet merchant marine and fisheries industries use several sailing ships as well as more modern ships dedicated to personnel training.

training ship. Over the last several years naval protocol visits also have been exchanged between the Soviets and Britain, Canada, Sweden and France, as well as a number of other nations.

Thus, the Soviets are impressively visible, especially to those who need to use the sea for political, economic, and military purposes. The perceptions of Soviet naval and maritime prestige held by other nations have become a major factor in international relations.

In summary, Americans must keep a perspective when discussing the development, capabilities, and intentions of the Soviet Navy. We must be cautious of overstating, but, even more important, we must guard against understating the threat posed by the Soviet Navy both as a peacetime organization and a fighting force.

The Soviet Navy's first full-fledged aircraft carrier was the KIEV. Here her sistership MINSK is about to land a FORGER approaching over the fantail—note the spray being generated by the VTOL fighters' vertical lift engine.

# Section 4. Soviet Naval Hardware

*In the course of building our Navy, a great deal of attention was devoted and continues to be devoted to constantly maintaining all the elements comprising its combat strength in the most favorable combination, that is, as we have come to say today, to keep them balanced.*

Admiral of the Fleet of the Soviet Union
S.G. GORSHKOV

The Soviet government has made a tremendous investment in ships, aircraft, weapons, sensors, and related naval hardware during the past two decades. This investment has been directed toward producing a large ocean-going fleet that is, in many respects, innovative and highly capable. However, the missions of the Soviet Navy are somewhat different from those of Western navies, as are certain personnel traits, approaches to research, industrial base, and strategy, tactics and doctrine. Hence, Soviet naval hardware is, in many respects, different from "equivalent" U.S. naval systems.

## A. Surface Warships

The Soviet Navy maintains by far the world's largest fleet of principal surface combatants, patrol and coastal combatant forces. Admiral Gorshkov has stated that his surface ships are to provide "combat stability" for his prime war fighting forces, the submarines and naval aviation. The Soviets not only view their surface warships as necessary elements of a "balanced fleet," but also use their ocean-going warships as primary instruments for "showing the flag" throughout the world, providing a visible naval presence when necessary in support of Soviet foreign policy. Emphasis continues on multi-purpose, long-endurance ships more heavily armed with antisubmarine, antiair, and antiship weapons than most comparable ships in other navies.

Photographs and specifications of the surface warships are provided in Appendix C of this publication.

### Aviation Ships

The widely publicized KIEV class aircraft carriers are the largest warships ever completed by the Soviet Union.* After years of criticizing U.S. carriers as being obsolete and vulnerable, Soviet naval writers began to change their professed views in the late 1960s. Grudging praise of the flexibility and mobile power represented by the modern aircraft carriers, particularly those with nuclear power, began to creep into Soviet writings and has increased in recent years.

The Soviets now, for the first time, have a sea-based, fixed-wing aircraft in operation. The second KIEV class ship, the MINSK, is now in the Pacific Ocean Fleet, a third is fitting out, and a fourth is under construction.

There is evidence that the Soviets are planning to build a larger class of aircraft carrier than the KIEV. As to the form and purpose such a ship will take, there are several alternatives which can be debated. They vary from an enlargement on the present KIEV VSTOL/cruiser hybrid to a full blown *conventional take-off-and-landing* (CTOL) carrier similar to those operated by the U.S. Navy. A logical advance on the KIEV design could be nuclear-powered, of about 60,000 tons, with catapults, and an air wing of some 60 aircraft. Such a ship could join the fleet late in this decade.

---

*The Soviets originally classified the KIEV as a "large antisubmarine warfare cruiser," possibly because (1) that is her basic mission, (2) it was not politically acceptable to call any Soviet ship an aircraft carrier after years of deprecating remarks concerning Western carriers by Soviet military writers, (3) the Soviets may have wished to project this ship as another evolutionary development of their ASW cruiser program and not a copy of the Western aircraft carrier concept, or (4) the Soviets wished to circumvent some interpretations of the Montreux Convention which proscribe warship passage through the Turkish Straits. The Soviets appear to have now redesignated the KIEV class as some type of "aircraft carrying ship."

The Soviet Navy introduced several new and relatively radical cruiser and destroyer designs during the 1960s. At top is a KYNDA class cruiser with eight tubes for the long-range SS-N-3 antiship missile. The four-tube launchers are evident forward and aft of the ship's superstructure in this view. At center is a KASHIN class antiaircraft missile destroyer. This ship introduced gas turbine propulsion to large warships. At bottom is a KRESTA I class missile cruiser. The KRESTA I is a multi-mission ship, heavily armed and fitted with a variety of electronic systems.

The salient point to be understood with regard to Soviet aircraft carrier policy is that it appears that the Politburo has opted for yet another naval program which requires a long term commitment of extensive national resources and manpower. For whatever purpose or intent the Soviets pursue this high capital investment, the West cannot afford to ignore its future implications.

The KIEVs have an unusual design. They have a full load displacement of about 37,000 tons, are 900 feet long, have an angled flight deck some 600 feet long, and an island superstructure to starboard in the tradition of Western carriers. However, the forward part of these ships is similar to Soviet missile cruisers, with antiship, antisubmarine and antiaircraft missile launchers. They also have a profusion of more traditional weapons, electronic sensors, electronic warfare systems, and a number of advanced communications devices.

The lack of aircraft arresting wires and catapults on the flight deck limits the ships to helicopters and VSTOL aircraft. A mix of about 20 HORMONE helicopters, and 15 FORGER VTOL aircraft is a nominal air group, although this mix could be changed to meet varied mission requirements.

Although the primary mission of the KIEV class is stated by the Soviets as ASW, the ships also have a powerful antiship capability in their cruise missile battery. They have eight large launching tubes, with reloads for SS-N-12 missiles, which are an improvement over the older SS-N-3 antiship missiles. The HORMONE B helicopter has been seen aboard the KIEV class, with that helicopter being capable of providing over-the-horizon targeting information for the SS-N-12 missiles (which have a maximum range of some 300 nautical miles). Most of the embarked HORMONE helicopters are for ASW.

The FORGER has been observed operating in the antiship and nominal air defense roles. Depending on Soviet intentions, the aircraft might also be capable of ground attack, reconnaissance or other support roles. To date these aircraft have shown little inclination to stray any distance from the "Bird Farm". Tactical VSTOL technology is in its infancy with only FORGER and the British-designed HARRIER in service in significant numbers.* It is evident that this type of aircraft is destined to be widely deployed in a number of navies of the world. Although this first Soviet effort appears to be only VTOL capable and is relatively limited when com-

pared to other front-line tactical aircraft, it is important to remember that it represents the beginnings of a most significant and growing trend in the Soviet Navy—sea-based, fixed-wing air power. As this power grows, the Soviet Navy will present opponents with a new range of threats, which in turn will tend to limit further those options available to Western naval commanders in a confrontation.

The KIEV is a second generation class of Soviet "aviation ship," following the helicopter carrier-missile cruisers MOSKVA and LENINGRAD, which were completed in 1967 and 1968, respectively. These earlier ships also were of innovative design, being essentially missile cruisers forward with a clear flight deck aft for operating up to 18 HORMONE antisubmarine helicopters. The latter ships are rated as "antisubmarine cruisers" by the Soviet Navy and have been used primarily in that role as well as serving as flagships.

Although helicopters are their main weapon, the MOSKVA class ships also have antiaircraft and antisubmarine missiles, ASW rockets, torpedo tubes, and guns. Advanced radars, sonars (both hull mounted and variable depth), and advanced electronic warfare equipment are fitted in the ships. They thus combine the full weapons-sensor suite of a guided missile cruiser with the capacity to handle a large squadron of ASW helicopters.

### Cruisers

Late in 1962 the Soviets sent a new type of warship to sea, the first KYNDA class guided missile cruiser. This ship is of small cruiser size, displacing about 5,500 tons full load, and measuring 465 feet in length. The four KYNDA class ships are armed with antiaircraft missiles, multi-purpose guns, and antisubmarine weapons.

Most significant is the main battery of the KYNDAs: eight tubes for the SS-N-3 antiship cruise missile and eight reload missiles in the ship's superstructure. With a maximum operational range of some 250 nautical miles the SS-N-3 is one of the world's longest-range operational weapons of its kind for use against ships. To insure accuracy when fired at ranges beyond the horizon (about 25 miles), the SS-N-3 requires midcourse guidance. Still, the missile allows a Soviet warship, so equipped, to outrange every Allied warship except for an aircraft carrier. Thus, Admiral Gorshkov attempted to counter the U.S. superiority in aircraft carriers with another type of warship rather than compete in a category where the United States had overwhelming superiority.

---

*The HARRIER is flown by the Royal Air Force, with the AV-8A version in service with the U.S. Marine Corps and the Spanish Navy.

After producing the four KYNDA class ships, in 1967 Soviet yards began building the KRESTA I class of slightly larger dimensions (7,500 tons and 510 feet). In this ship, the Soviets reduced the number of long-range SS-N-3 launchers from eight to four, but increased the twin antiaircraft missile launchers from one to two, and added a helicopter hangar. This permits the KRESTA I to maintain a HORMONE helicopter on board to provide missile targeting or other services.

The KRESTA I was apparently an interim class, pending the final development of an ASW cruiser design, and only four ships were built. The next cruiser off the Soviet building ways was the slightly larger KRESTA II.

With the KRESTA II class the Soviets changed the main weapon from the long-range SS-N-3 to eight launchers for the SS-N-14 ASW missile with a range of about 25 miles. This missile change apparently reflected the Soviet shift in missions discussed earlier, from purely anticarrier to antisubmarine and selective sea control. In addition, the KRESTA II has improved antiaircraft missiles and more advanced electronics. Ten of the KRESTA II class ships were completed from 1970 to 1978.

Another new missile cruiser was introduced in 1973 with completion of the first ship of the KARA class. The size trend in surface warships continued, with this ship having a displacement of 9,700 tons and a length of about 570 feet. Again, there were improvements in weapon and sensor capabilities, and there also was a concomitant increase of operating range with the larger size, demonstrating the expanding horizons of Soviet maritime interests.

The Soviets' first nuclear powered surface warship, KIROV, on her initial sea trials in the Baltic in the summer of 1980. This ship is the largest combatant built in the world since World War II (excluding aircraft carriers). It carries 20 new type long-range cruise missiles, plus 12 vertical launch tubes for a new SAM system. This ship is equipped with numerous other weapons and sensors and is capable of carrying several helicopters aft.

The KRIVAK class missile frigate, also powered by gas turbines, is primarily an ASW ship. However, the KRIVAKs have torpedo tubes and guns, with later ships than the one seen here having two guns of 100mm caliber aft in place of the four 76mm AA weapons in twin gun mounts. These ships lack the helicopter facilities in contemporary U.S. destroyers and frigates.

The KARA class ships are gas-turbine powered and are more heavily armed than any similar sized ships of other navies. The KARA's main weapons are the same as in a KRESTA II, but with two additional launchers for short range antiaircraft missiles, a heavier gun battery, and the addition of a variable depth sonar. Seven KARA class cruisers are in service and construction has apparently been completed.

Besides the succeeding classes of missiles cruisers produced by the Soviet yards since the early 1960s, the Soviet Navy has retained twelve of the older SVERD-LOV class large cruisers built during the 1950s. Most of these ships remain in active service with an all-gun armament (12 six-inch guns). It is interesting to note that while almost all of the gun cruisers in the world's other navies have been retired, the Soviets continue to modernize and operate these ships.

One SVERDLOV class cruiser has a "refitted" twin launcher for medium-range antiaircraft missiles in place of a six-inch gun turret, while two other ships have been converted to "command ship" configurations. Amidships these two ships have been fitted with additional spaces for an admiral and his staff, satellite communications systems have been installed, and short-range missile launchers and rapid-fire "Gatling" guns are provided for antiaircraft/missile defense. These two modified SVERDLOVs, as well as the aviation ships, provide

extensive communications, especially for command and control of operations. Several other SVERD-LOVs have recently been modernized as well, so the class is expected to remain in service for some years to come.

Cruiser type warships are currently being built in the Soviet Union at the rate of approximately two per year. U.S. cruiser construction, in comparison, has averaged one ship every 2½ years over the past decade.

The Soviets are currently embarked on a most ambitious surface warship construction program. At least four new classes of cruiser or large destroyer size warships have been identified under construction in Soviet yards, totalling about a dozen new hulls with more anticipated.

The most impressive ship of this new generation of combatants is the Soviet's first nuclear powered warship. This ship, and a sister, are being built in Leningrad. It is estimated to be some 23,000 full load displacement tons, which will make it, apart from aircraft carriers, the largest warship built in the world since World War II. The first of this class, KIROV, joined the fleet in late 1980. This ship carries 20 of a new type cruise missile of about the same size as the SS-N-12 but probably with improved performance. Additionally, KIROV has 12 launchers for a new advanced surface-to-air missile system plus two shorter range SAM launchers, two

100mm guns, two ASW missile launchers, Gatling guns, torpedoes and several helicopters.

The other three new warship classes are estimated to vary in size from 7,500 to 14,000 displacement tons. Reports of armament vary by class and include new types of surface-to-air and cruise missiles as well as large guns.

One of these ships, the guided missile destroyer SOVREMENNYY, built in Zhdanov Shipyard, Leningrad, from whence the KRESTAs came, is conducting sea trails and is expected to join the fleet soon. Although her main armament is not installed, it appears provisions have been made for two large gun mounts, two new type SAM launchers and four or more antiship cruise missile launchers. This ship is already equipped with two short range SAM launchers, four Gatling guns, torpedoes and a helicopter hanger.

The function for which each of these four new warship classes has been designed will remain speculative until equipments and employment patterns are discerned. What is definite, is that the Soviets continue to demonstrate their commitment to expanding naval capabilities with ambitious, extensive programs such as these.

## Destroyers/Frigates

Since World War II, the Soviets have added five new classes of destroyers to their active fleet. As in the West, Soviet destroyers have experienced an evolutionary growth in the size of their destroyers.

The first post-World War II destroyer construction program produced the SKORYY class. Over 70 of these ships were built and a number still remain in active service. They are rarely seen beyond Soviet coastal waters. Fourteen of these ships have been transferred to Egypt, Poland, and Indonesia.

In the early 1950s and early 1960s the Soviet Navy successively introduced the KOTLIN class gun destroyer (27 built), the KILDIN class antiship missile destroyer (4 built), and the KRUPNYY class antiship missile destroyer (8 built). The KOTLINs have received various modifications over the years, including surface-to-air missiles added to nine (one since transferred to Poland). The KILDINs were built on KOTLIN hulls and three have also been modified in recent years, including the installation of four improved STYX antiship missiles. All eight of the KRUPNYYs have had their early antiship missile systems replaced by eight 57mm guns forward and a twin SAM launcher fitted aft, and additional ASW weapons and equipments were added. Thus reconfigured, these ships are now called the KANIN class.

From early 1963 through 1967 Soviet shipyards delivered 20 KASHIN class guided missile destroyers. These are ships of 4,500 tons and 476 feet in length. They are armed with two antiaircraft missile launchers, antisubmarine rocket launchers, five torpedo tubes, four 76mm multi-purpose guns, and mine rails. Five have been subsequently fitted with four short-range, antiship missiles (SS-N-2), and variable depth sonar. In the fall of 1974, one KASHIN class ship sank in the Black Sea, apparently as the result of an internal fire and explosion.

Their most distinctive feature is four large funnels in pairs for the tandem gas-turbine power

The brand new SOVREMENNYY class missile destroyer (translates to *modern*) shown here in the Baltic on its initial sea trials in the summer of 1980. Note that the primary weapons (probably new surface-to-air and antiship missile systems as well as a new type gun mount both fore and aft) are not yet installed. Besides a collapsible helicopter hangar, this ship has fitted four "Gatling" guns, two SA-N-4 launchers, torpedo tubes and two ASW rocket launchers. As several other ships of this class are under construction, this class no doubt will be in series production through the mid-eighties. At 7500 tons it is about the size of the U.S. Navy's SPRUANCE class DD.

plants. These were the world's first large warships with gas turbines and they give the KASHINs an estimated top speed of over 36 knots for brief periods.

Marine gas turbines provide a high horse-power-to-weight ratio, and are easy to maintain and replace. They can go from "cold-iron" to full power operations in a few minutes, and can rapidly accelerate, unlike steam turbines that require a steam buildup for acceleration.

Soviet success with the KASHIN propulsion system led to gas turbine application in the smaller KRIVAK class missile frigates and the larger KARA class cruisers.

The Soviet Navy has a large number of frigates which operate with fleet formations on the high seas as antisubmarine escorts and as coastal patrol ships. The KRIVAK class missile frigate, the first of which went to sea in 1970, now numbers about 30 ships and construction continues. These ships displace about 3,600 tons and have an overall length of 405 feet. The KRIVAKs are armed with both antisubmarine and antiaircraft missiles. They have a four-tube launcher for the SS-N-14 ASW missiles and two twin reloadable launchers for the SA-N-4 short-range SAM missile. In addition, the ship has antisubmarine rockets, eight torpedo tubes, mine rails, and four 76mm guns. In some of the later ships two single guns of 100mm size replace the 76mm weapon; these ships have been designated the KRIVAK II class. The ship's sensors are complemented by advanced electronic systems, including both hull-mounted and variable depth sonars. The KRIVAKs

have been built at a rate of three to four per year.

Few of the destroyers built since World War II have been scrapped. The great majority are still in active service, with SKORYYs providing most of a small reserve force.

The remainder of the approximately 135 frigates in the Soviet Navy are smaller types of the MIRKA, PETYA, and GRISHA classes which are each about 1,200 to 1,600 tons in displacement (about the size of United States World War II destroyer escort). In addition, there are a number of the older RIGAs (1,500 tons). The first units of a new class, the 2,100 ton KONI, have recently been delivered to the East German Navy and Yugoslavia. Of the smaller frigates, only the GRISHA and KONI class remain in production.

Although these frigates are smaller than most Western frigates, they nonetheless deploy regularly to the Mediterranean and Indian Ocean where they are an integral part of the permanent Soviet squadrons operating in those seas.

## B. Small Combatants

The Soviet Union operates large numbers of small combatants—missile, torpedo, patrol, and mine craft.

Probably the most publicized of these craft are the OSA missile boats which displace some 215 tons and are 129 feet long. Each OSA carries four launchers for the SS-N-2 STYX missile, which has a range of

A NATYA class ocean minesweeper. The Soviets operate almost 400 mine warfare ships and craft as well as maintain what is estimated to be by far the world's largest stockpile of mines.

about 25 miles. The OSA II boats carry improved missiles which have a range of over 40 miles. With a sustained speed of 34 knots and two rapid-fire, twin 30mm gun mounts, the OSAs are potent ship killers. About 120 OSAs are currently in Soviet service and over 125 have been transferred to other navies (as have some 60 of the earlier, two-missile KOMAR missile boats).

In 1969 the Soviets introduced the NANUCHKA class guided missile patrol combatant into service. This ship displaces amost 900 tons and is 194 feet long. The NANUCHKA I has a twin SA-N-4 anti-aircraft missile launcher forward and a twin 57mm gun aft. A later variant, the NANUCHKA III, have a single 57mm and a 30mm Gatling gun. The main battery consists of six tubes for the SS-N-9 missile. This antiship weapon has a maximum range estimated at about 60 miles. Several modified versions of this ship, NANUCHKA II, carrying four SS-N-2 missiles have been sold to India.

A new hydrofoil missile boat, the SARANCHA, has been operating for several years. This gas turbine powered craft is smaller than the NANUCHKA and mounts only four SS-N-9 missiles, plus an SA-N-4 missile system and a Gatling gun.

Besides the aforementioned ships, the Soviet Navy has large numbers of a variety of classes of small combatants: patrol boats, torpedo boats, hydrofoil patrol boats, submarine chasers, gunboats, and river monitors. The maritime arm of the KGB

BABOCHKA class PCSH. A gas turbine powered, hydrofoil, sub chaser which is just entering the Soviet inventory. This boat appears to be armed with a number of torpedos plus two "Gatling" guns. As with larger surface warships the Soviets are producing a number of new classes of smaller combatants.

(the state security police) also operates several classes of frigates and small combatants.

Several new classes of these types of ships have been observed and include the MATKA class missile equipped hydrofoil gunboat, the TARANTUL missile gunboat, and the BABOUCHKA class submatine chaser.

The Soviet Navy's mine warfare force is the largest in the world. Over 200 ocean and coastal minesweepers, plus a number of minesweeping boats, make up the active force. The classes of ocean minesweepers (540 to 900 tons) includes the NATYA, YURKA, and T-43 classes; and the coastal minesweepers (200 to 400 tons) include the SONYA, ZHENYA, VANYA, and SASHA classes.

TURYA class PTH. The hydrofoil torpedo boats are armed with four torpedo tubes, a twin 57mm dual purpose gun aft, and a quad 23mm mount forward. These boats usually operate in the littoral seas of the USSR.

The Soviet Navy uses these mine warfare ships for a variety of tasks besides their primary function, such as patrol and picket duties. Besides this large force of minewarfare ships, it is estimated the Soviets also maintain the world's largest stock of mines of numerous different types. The Russians have a long history of interest in mine warfare and continue to actively pursue all aspects of mining, both offensively and defensively.

## C. Submarines

The Soviet Navy long has been a world leader in operating submarines. Beginning in the late 1930s, the Soviet Navy generally has had more undersea craft than any other navy.

Today the Soviet submarine force numbers about 360 units. In discussing them one must address three specific categories:

- Torpedo attack submarines—that attack an enemy surface warship or submarine using torpedoes or missile delivered ASW weapons.
- Cruise missiles submarines—that fire large antiship cruise missiles as well as torpedoes.
- Strategic ballistic missile submarines—armed with vertically-launched, nuclear-tipped missiles for strategic targets.

The Soviet Navy is operating a total of about 165 nuclear powered submarines compared to some 115 in the U.S. Navy.

### Attack Submarines

The Soviet Navy operates about 210 attack submarines. Most are diesel-electric powered and many are of recent construction. A growing percentage of these submarines are nuclear powered. About 40 of the torpedo attack submarines are nuclear powered, being of the NOVEMBER, ECHO, VICTOR, and

Aircraft and submarines armed with cruise missiles are the principal antiship forces of the Soviet Navy. At top is a CHARLIE I class submarine which has eight submerged-launched SS-N-7 missiles and, below, an ECHO II with eight SS-N-3 missiles fired from the surface. Both of these classes are nuclear powered and can operate in virtually any ocean area.

ALFA classes. The last is believed to be the fastest submarine in service today. An improved VICTOR class is now in production and the small, high-speed, deep-diving ALFA class may well be in series production. The Soviet Navy continues to build diesel powered submarines, the FOXTROT class for overseas sales (Indian, Libya and Cuba) and the new TANGO class. Soviet writers have noted that diesel-electric submarines offer a quiet-running, highly capable platform which can operate in shallower waters than the larger nuclear powered boats and at a fraction of the construction cost.

The prime weapons of these attack submarines are antisubmarine and antiship torpedoes; however, mines also can be carried. The newer submarines have a rocket-propelled ASW weapon as well.

## Cruise Missile Submarines

Building on German experiments during World War II, both the U.S. and Soviet navies experimented with missile-launching submarines after World War II. In the U.S. Navy this effort evolved into the REGULUS cruise missile program. Although the REGULUS could be used against ships, the lack of significant Soviet surface threat in the 1950s led to American development of the REGULUS as a strategic weapon for strikes against bases, ports and cities. The POLARIS technology quickly overtook the REGULUS in this role.

The Soviet Navy developed cruise missile submarines in the 1950s for strategic attack and as a part of a strategy to counter U.S. aircraft carriers. Initially, existing submarines were converted to fire the long-range SS-N-3 missile. Then, newer submarines designed to carry the SS-N-3 joined the Soviet fleet —the diesel powered JULIETT class and the nuclear powered ECHO I and II classes.

After producing about 50 submarines of the JULIETT and ECHO classes, the Soviets completed the first CHARLIE I class SSGN in 1968 with the improved CHARLIE II following several years later. These nuclear powered submarines can fire eight antiship cruise missiles while remaining submerged at a range of some 30 miles from an intended target. Although the CHARLIE missile range is less than that of submarines armed with the SS-N-3, the latter submarines must surface before firing their missiles. The underwater launch capability of the CHARLIE makes this craft one of the most potent antiship submarines in service today. All of these cruise missile submarines also have standard torpedo tubes.

The Soviets have launched a new class of very large, nuclear powered cruise missile submarine, the OSCAR class. It is estimated that this behemoth will carry 20 to 30 of a new generation cruise missile perhaps similar to those installed on the Soviets' new nuclear powered cruiser, KIROV.

The Soviet Navy's cruise missile submarines and their missile-armed bombers form the greatest threat to Allied naval forces operating on the high seas. This is especially so when within range of Soviet air bases where the Soviets can launch coordinated attacks using not only reconnaissance aircraft to provide target data for submarine-launched missiles, but also their extensive force of naval and air force missile equipped bombers.

The 34 YANKEE class strategic missile submarines completed since 1967 were the "second generation" Soviet SSBNs. More than 30 later DELTA I/II/III submarines are now at sea, with some sources indicating a still more advanced SSBN, the TYPHOON class, also being under construction. An intensive submarine missile development effort has accompanied their construction.

## Ballistic Missile Submarines

The development of nuclear weapons led to another role for the submarine, that of strategic or ballistic missile attack against land targets. Submarines are valuable in this role because the difficulty of their detection in the ocean depths makes them highly survivable against hostile attack.

As discussed earlier, the Soviets began converting existing diesel powered submarines in the mid-1950s to fire short-range Submarine Launched Ballistic Missiles (SLBMs). Then, in the early 1960s, the GOLF class diesel and HOTEL class nuclear SLBM submarines were completed. These submarines were initially limited by mechanical difficulties, short-range missiles, and the requirement for surfacing to launch their missiles. (Most of these submarines were later provided with a submerged missile launch capability and improved weapons.)

Today, the Soviet Navy has an SLBM force that exceeds that of the U.S. Navy in numbers of submarines and in missiles. By the end of 1974, the Soviet Navy had 34 of the YANKEE class SSBNs in service, each carrying 16 nuclear-tipped missiles with a range of at least 1,300 nautical miles (later increased to about 1,600 miles). During 1973 the first of the larger DELTA class submarines was completed. The early DELTAs displace some 11,000 tons submerged and have an overall length of about 460 feet. The DELTA I has 12 tubes for the SS-N-8 missile with an estimated range of over 4,000 nautical miles. The DELTA II and III carries 16 SS-N-8 or SS-N-18 SLBMs, respectively, and are about 50 feet longer than the DELTA I. The DELTA III class is the largest submarine presently in operation (about 13,000 tons submerged displacement), but will soon be surpassed by the U.S. Navy's OHIO class SSBN (about 18,000 tons). The SS-N-18 missile is the first Soviet SLBM to have multiple independently targeted re-entry vehicles (MIRV), carrying as many as seven warheads which can be aimed at separate targets. The SS-N-18 is more accurate, if not longer ranged than the SS-N-8. The SS-N-17 is the first solid propellant SLBM built by the Soviets and to date is carried on only one converted YANKEE (designated YANKEE II). This missile uses a post-boost vehicle which would allow it to carry a MIRV package. This new missile probably has increased accuracy and range capabilities compared to the SS-N-6 carried on the YANKEE I class. To keep within the SALT I treaty limits of 62 "modern" SSBNs, the Soviets are removing the missile tubes from a YANKEE for each DELTA III now added to the fleet.

In the fall of 1980 the Soviets launched a new strategic ballistic missile submarine at Severodvinsk shipyard in the Northern USSR. It is estimated this is the initial unit of a new class of large nuclear powered submarine capable of launching long-range strategic missiles.

This new submarine could well be the "Typhoon" referred to by the Soviets in the past, which has prompted the West to designate it the TYPHOON class. Initial information indicates this gigantic submarine is at least twice the tonnage of the DELTA III class SSBN, the largest submarines ever put to sea. By contrast the U.S. Navy's OHIO class SSBN, scheduled for sea trials in 1981, is about 18,000 tons submerged and will carry 24 TRIDENT missiles.

With the "state of the art" achieved in other Soviet strategic missile programs it is assumed the missile for this new submarine will be more capable than the SS-N-18 carried on the DELTA III; possibly having either, or all of, greater range, better accuracy, higher payload and more warheads. The DELTA III submarines can today cover most U.S. targets from the relative security of their home waters—the TYPHOON will certainly have no less capability.

# D. Aircraft

Soviet Naval Aviation (SNA) is completely subordinate to the Soviet Navy, with regiments being assigned to each of the four fleets under an aviation officer who reports directly to the fleet commander. The naval air arm consists of over 1,300 aircraft, most of which are based ashore except for helicopters assigned to various cruisers, and the helicopters and VTOL aircraft that fly from the KIEV class aircraft carriers.

Although they are career naval officers, aviators in the Soviet Navy have the same rank structure as the Soviet Air Force, which also provides their basic training.

Soviet naval aviation currently has four basic missions:

## Reconnaissance and Surveillance

Naval aircraft are employed in long-range reconnaissance ("recce") and ocean surveillance, with some aircraft equipped to provide mid-course target data for antiship missiles launched "over the horizon" from surface ships, submarines, and other aircraft. Reconnaissance aircraft now in use include about 50 of the larger BEAR D turbo-prop planes;

The Soviet Navy flies over 500 twin-jet BADGER aircraft in the missile strike, reconnaissance, electronic, tanker, and training roles. This BADGER was photographed while looking over a U.S. carrier. With the BADGER is a U.S. Navy F-4 PHANTOM fighter.

about 100 twin-jet BADGER aircraft, with about the same performance as the now-discarded U.S. B-47 jet bombers; and a few BLINDER jet aircraft that have a supersonic dash speed. Additionally, the MAY maritime patrol aircraft are used for surveillance and reconnaissance missions.

These aircraft and others flown by SNA are described in Appendix D.

## Antiship Strike

The prime striking force of Soviet Naval Aviation consists of some 290 twin-jet BADGER aircraft which are fitted to carry one or two of several types of antiship cruise missiles with "stand-off" ranges varying from 55 to over 250 miles. Some missiles have variable flight paths to help penetrate ship defenses and various homing techniques. All these missiles are assessed to be nuclear capable or carry a high explosive warhead of about 1,000 to 2,000 pounds.

Soviet Naval Aviation also flies the twin-jet BACKFIRE, a supersonic aircraft with variable-swing wings. This plane carries stand-off missiles and is slowly replacing the BADGER in strike squadrons. The Navy is receiving this aircraft at about the same rate as Long-Range Aviation (the strategic bombing force) and the inventory has climbed to over 50 aircraft. The BACKFIRE greatly increases the capability and extends the range at which SNA strike aircraft can attack Western surface forces such as air-

craft carrier or amphibious task groups.

The introduction of aircraft carriers and FORGER aircraft gives the SNA another dimension of antiship strike. The FORGER can be fitted with short-range air-to-surface missiles, rockets, or bombs for use against ship or shore targets.

The FITTER fighter-bomber has been introduced into SNA over the last several years. These aircraft are assigned to the Baltic Fleet primarily to provide

A FORGER VTOL fighter sits on the deck of the carrier KIEV. Note intake panel behind cockpit which covers the lift engines when the aircraft is in horizontal flight.

antiship strike and close support to amphibious operations in the Baltic.

In addition to naval aircraft armed with antiship missiles, certain BEAR and BADGER bombers of Soviet Long-Range Aviation can be used for attacks against shipping, and these aircrft regularly participate in naval exercises. Most of these strike aircraft can be refueled in-flight by naval BADGERs fitted as tankers as well as by Long-Range Aviation tankers.

## Antisubmarine

The Soviet Navy has a large force of fixed-wing aircraft and helicopters configured for submarine detection and attack. This force currently includes about 30 ASW configured BEAR F aircraft, 50 MAY turbo-prop aircraft that resemble the U.S. P-3 ORI-ON, and 100 MAIL twin-engine flying boat aircraft. Only the BEAR F appears to be still in production. These aircraft operate from Soviet land bases to search out seaward areas for foreign submarines. They carry a variety of detection equipment as well as ASW depth bombs and torpedoes.

An increasing number of antisubmarine helicopters are being flown by the Soviet Navy. The HOR-MONE A, a twin turboshaft helicopter, is flown from the newer Soviet cruisers, as well as from the helicopter carriers MOSKVA and LENINGRAD and the KIEV class aircraft carriers. An ASW version of the HIP helicopter, which has been named the HAZE by Western intelligence, has been entering SNA inventory. Because of its larger size, it is unlikely to be used on existing Soviet warships. It is more likely

a replacement for the older shore-based, HOUND ASW helicopters. The HAZE is reported to be now operating in all four fleets.

The aircraft carrier KIEV operates both ASW and missile targeting variants (the "B" model) of the HORMONE. A utility version (HORMONE C) is also carried for miscellaneous missions including search-and-rescue. From extensive experimental work in VSTOL technology, the Soviets developed the FORGER VTOL tactical aircraft; both the single and two-seat versions have been sighted on the KIEV. This aircraft is estimated to have about the same speed as the U.S. Marine Corps' AV-8A HAR-RIER VSTOL, but does not appear to have similar range or maneuvering capabilities.

During their four years of limited operations of the FORGER the Soviets have provided some indication of the role this aircraft is intended to play, as it has been employed primarily as a basic flight training and surface strike aircraft. It is likely the plane is designed for several roles such as fighter defense, antiship strike, reconnaissance, close air support ashore and possibly even ASW support. Its capabilities in any of these roles are limited relative to Western carrier aircraft.

But one must understand that this is the first attempt by the Soviets at fixed wing carrier operations —their "Model T" compared to future developments. What must be emphasized is *the trend;* where the Soviets had "zero" capability in this area 10 years ago, now they have some. One can be assured that the Soviet Navy will be operating many more carrier-based aircraft with much greater capabilities ten years from now. As Soviet carrier air

An AIST class air cushion vehicle provides high speed across the beach assault for Soviet Naval Infantry. The Soviet Navy is by far the world's largest operator of surface effect ships. There are currently three different classes of air cushion vehicles in the naval inventory—the AIST is the largest.

capabilities increase so do the seapower options available to the Politburo.

### Support

The Soviet Naval Aviation also operates some 125 transport and utility aircraft of various types. Although basic and advanced training are provided by the Soviet Air Forces, maritime operational training is accomplished within the Navy. The SNA retains a number of transports to provide a logistics capability to better meet the Navy's priority needs.

In recent years Soviet Naval Aviation has been gaining in strength and prestige. Recent manifestations include the construction of KIEV class carriers, the introduction of the BACKFIRE bomber, the elevation of the commander of Soviet Naval Aviation to a rank of Marshal, and the various references in Admiral Gorshkov's writings as to the importance of his air arm.

## E. Amphibious Forces

Another area of continuing development in the Soviet Navy has been amphibious assault forces. Within the Soviet Navy, "marines" are known as "naval infantry". Since it was reformed in the early 1960s, this force has received considerable publicity in the Soviet press and is bannered as an elite combat force. Today there are an estimated 12,000 Soviet marines, mostly allocated to the four fleets. (The U.S. Marine Corps, by comparison, numbers about 185,000 men and women.)

The mission of the Soviet marines and hence their organization and equipment differ somewhat from that of the U.S. Marine Corps. The Soviets are not able to conduct extensive independent operations as our marines are. Instead, they spearhead amphibious landings for other ground forces and hold captured beachheads against counterattack, carry out "prolonged" river crossings and defend naval bases.

Although described as "light" infantry, the Soviet marine force is highly mechanized and is equipped with tracked and wheeled amphibious vehicles, including tanks and armored personnel carriers.

Amphibious lift for the naval infantry is provided primarily by IVAN ROGOV class LPDs, ALLIGATOR class and ROPHUCHA class LSTs, and POLNOCNY class LSMs. The Soviet amphibious forces exercise regularly in their respective fleet areas and regularly deploy to the Mediterranean, off West Africa, and the Indian Ocean. The Soviet Navy has about 25 LSTs and over 60 LSMs, plus numerous lesser landing craft and air cushion vehicles for amphibious operations.

The Soviet Navy is now the world's largest operator of military air cushion vehicles for which development continues. There are three classes currently in use: The GUS, LEBED and large AIST class.

Although small by comparison to the U.S. Marine Corps (the Soviet Naval Infantry is the second largest marine force in the world), the potential power of even a few hundred Soviet marines afloat in any given area during a crisis provides the Soviet Union with a valuable politico-military tool. For operations at some distance from the U.S.S.R., the Soviet ability to conduct an amphibious assault is limited to landings against positions where little or no opposition is expected ashore or in the seaward approaches of the landing area. But the Soviets have in hand, or are developing, the elements necessary to provide a formidable projection into distant waters, if that is their choice. These include the improvement in assault lift capability, the expansion of a large administrative lift ability designed into certain ships of the Merchant Marine, the retention of a substantial gunfire support strength in the older cruisers and destroyers, development of sea-based tactical air power, and a steadily improving underway replenishment capability. The Soviet Navy's ability to project tactical power ashore at some distance from the Soviet littoral may be part of Admiral Gorshkov's "grand plan" in achieving a "balanced fleet".

## F. Auxiliaries

As befitting a fleet of its size, the Soviet Navy operates a large number of auxiliaries, including many types and classes performing a myriad of function in various roles. The total of all categories approximates 760 ships.

One area in which the Soviets have lagged behind the Western navies is that of underway replenishment. The Soviets provide the great percentage of replenishment and routine maintenance to their deployed units in open anchorages in international waters. Although such activities appear more than adequate in peacetime operations, this mode of support would be most vulnerable in times of conflict. The Soviet Navy has slowly been improving their capabilities in the area of underway replenishment. Today, of 85 replenishment ships about 20 are capable of alongside refueling. The BORIS CHILIKIN class AORs and the new BEREZINA AOR are the most capable of these types. The Soviets still extensively use the astern method of refueling, which requires the participants to proceed at slow speed or remain dead in the water. The Soviets also rely on the merchant marine to provide a substantial percentage of their fuel at sea.

BEREZINA is a 40,000 ton multi-purpose replenishment ship, similar in size, appearance and capabilities to our WICHITA class AORs. It is armed with guns and missiles and appears to be designed to operate as an integral part of a battle group. Besides various liquids, this ship can also transfer solid stores, including missiles, while underway. The ship has a two helicopter hangar capacity. Although only one of this class has been built, it is expected the Soviets will continue to develop and improve this type of auxiliary.

Other auxiliaries which deploy regularly are material and fleet support ships such as: large submarine tenders (AS), which also serve the fleet as command and general maintenance ships, missile tenders (AEM), water transports (AW), (many Soviet ships suffer from small fresh water evaporator capacity), stores ships (AF), repair ships (AR), ocean tugs (ATA), etc. In addition to auxiliaries providing direct support to the fleet, other auxiliaries of the Soviet Navy are plying the "seven seas" in virtually every corner of the world in any given day. These include such types as intelligence, survey and research, and space event support ships.

The Soviets also use auxiliaries extensively for fleet maintenance and support in many of their home operating bases, in lieu of extensive fixed base assets ashore.

The Soviets rely to a fair extent on their Warsaw Pact allies, particularly Poland and East Germany to construct naval auxiliaries. A more recent example of this is the building of two large hospital ships in Poland; the Soviets have not had any such ships for years. The reasons the Soviets feel they need such ships at this juncture are speculative. Finland, West Germany, Sweden, Japan and the United Kingdom have also built auxiliaries now serving in the Soviet Navy.

## G. Surveillance, Intelligence, and Communications

The Soviet Navy's increased operations have been matched by quantitative and by qualitative increases in related surveillance, intelligence, and communications activities. The most obvious manifestation of this aspect of Soviet naval activity has

The newest class replenishment ship (AOR) is the 40,000 ton BEREZINA. This large ship is equipped to move both liquids and solids while steaming alongside either to port or starboard. It also carries two helicopters for vertical replenishment of stores and personnel. This ship is armed with a twin launcher SA-N-4 SAM and two twin 57mm guns.

been the extensive operations of passive intelligence collection or "spy" ships.

These ships are known as "intelligence collectors" and are designated as AGIs; more than 50 of them are in service. They are often depicted in the press as disguised fishing trawlers. However, they are clearly identifiable as naval intelligence ships, manned by naval personnel, flying the Soviet naval ensign, and easily identified by their varied and unusual electronic antennas. Some of the AGIs are of modified trawler design, others of modified survey-research ship design, and a number are built-for-the-purpose of intelligence "factories." The latter of the PRIMORYE class displace about 4,000 tons. A new large AGI, the BALZAM class, joined the Soviet fleet in 1980—this ship displaces over 5,000 tons.

Soviet AGI-type ships normally keep watch off the U.S. missile submarine bases of Holy Loch, Scotland, and Guam in the Marianas. An AGI normally operates off the Southeastern coast of the United States, a position that permits surveillance of the submarine bases at Charleston, South Carolina, or Kings Bay, Georgia; the aircraft carrier operating areas off Virginia or Florida; or the missile activity at Cape Kennedy. AGIs regularly dog NATO and U.S. naval forces during exercises and are usually present in most Soviet-United States naval confrontations.

The concept of operating ships exclusively for overt intelligence tasks was discarded by the U.S. Navy after the misfortunes of the USS PUEBLO (captured by the North Koreans) and the USS LIBERTY (severely damaged by Israeli air and naval attack back in the 1960s). Significantly, U.S. Navy ships employed in this passive intelligence role during that period were converted World War II-built cargo ships, whereas the Soviet vessels are of relatively recent construction. Over the last several years, the Soviets have armed a number of their AGIs with small surface-to-air missiles.

In addition to AGIs, the Soviet Navy, like other major navies, employs surface warships, submarines and aircraft for intelligence collection.

Increasingly, the Soviet Navy is also employing advanced satellite surveillance systems. Recent naval-associated surveillance satellites have improved collection rates and processing capabilities. These include electronic intelligence (ELINT) satellites (that can "lock on" to electronic signals from Western warships to provide location information), radar surveillance satellites and photographic satellites. The ELINT and radar satellites can provide almost real-time detection and possibly some weapon-guidance capability.

Satellite surveillance systems are in extensive use by the Soviet armed forces. According to published reports, the Soviets apparently employed reconnaissance satellites to keep track of the 1973 war in the Middle East. Four reconnaissance satellites were orbited during the 12-day period in early October, apparently related to the Arab-Israeli war that erupted on October 6, 1973. Indications are that the Soviets increased their satellite collection during the more recent Iranian and Afghan crises.

Satellites are also employed by the Soviet Navy for long-range communications. A number of Soviet warships and support ships have satellite communication equipment, including the KIEV class carrier and the two SVERDLOV class cruisers that were modified to serve as command and communication ships in remote ocean areas. These ships are fitted with advanced communications equipment, command and control spaces, and accommodations for an admiral and staff. More recently the Soviets modified a GOLF class submarine for this same purpose.

The Soviet Navy has developed advanced conventional communication equipment for the tactical coordination of strike forces. For example, Soviet surface missile ships, missile-armed submarines, and aircraft are able to rapidly exchange targeting information and coordinate strikes against surface ship targets. During the large-scale OKEAN maneuvers of 1970 and 1975, the Soviets were observed to simulate several coordinated attacks against surface ships. In some phases of the multi-ocean exercise, naval bombers simultaneously flew simulated strike missions in both the North Atlantic and Western Pacific Oceans, with warships in the different oceans being attacked at the same moment. Now the Soviets conduct more extensive and complex exercises than in the past, particularly during the spring and summer periods.

This requirement for simultaneous strikes in widely separated ocean areas is part of the Soviet Navy's "short war" or "first salvo" concept discussed earlier in this publication.

Published Soviet reports describing OKEAN 1970 tell of the Navy Commander-in-Chief being able to communicate with major units anywhere in the world almost instantly, knowing that an order had been executed by a ship in a "matter of minutes," having available in real time the status of air, surface, and underwater situations, including friendly and enemy orders of battle, and being able to monitor "how the (ship) commander conducts a search and accurately judges the effectiveness of his actions."

## H. Other Warsaw Pact Navies

Four of the six non-Soviet Warsaw Pact (NSWP) countries have navies: Poland, the German Democratic Republic (GDR) (East Germany), Bulgaria and Rumania. These forces are designed primarily to operate in the coastal areas of their respective countries, and units are seldom seen outside of the Baltic Sea (Poland and the GDR) or the Black Sea (Bulgaria and Rumania).

The Baltic NSWP navies are by far the more capable in relation to those in the Black Sea, and it appears the former are much more integrated with the Soviet Navy in matters of Warsaw Pact operations than the latter. These navies have a proliferation of ship classes that are home-built or provided by the Soviets.

The Poles and Germans are excellent ship builders, and their navies have several classes of ships which are of indigenous design and construction. Examples of these are the FROSH class LST, LIBELLE class PTL and HAI class PG in the GDR Navy and the POLNOCNY class LSM and the OBLUZE class PCS in the Polish Navy. A number of amphibious ships and auxiliaries in the Soviet Navy were also built in Poland.

The Poles have a naval air arm which consists of about 90 helicopters, older MIG fighters and BEAGLE bombers. The GDR Navy operates a small contingent of ASW helicopters.

Poland has a well balanced navy which includes: four WHISKEY class submarines; a KOTLIN class DDG; a number of smaller combatants, including OSA class missile boats; a good size amphibious force; about 50 mine warfare ships and craft, plus a few auxiliaries. Although there are no marines in the Polish Navy, there is a dedicated "amphibious landing division" in the Polish Army which exercises with the navy's amphibious assault force.

The GDR Navy has no submarines or destroyers but does have two of the new KONI class frigates recently built by the Soviets. They also operate a large coastal patrol force including OSA class missile boats, an amphibious force able to lift the amphibious dedicated motorized rifle regiment in the GDR Army, and a coastal minesweeper group.

The Rumanian Navy consists mainly of 3 POTI class patrol escorts, about 66 coastal patrol craft, including a few OSAs, and a mine warfare force of approximately 32. Some of the Rumanian units were purchased from Communist China, another indication that the Rumanians do not collaborate as closely with the Soviets as the latter might wish.

The Bulgarian Navy has four submarines of the WHISKEY and ROMEO classes, two RIGA class frigates, three POTI class patrol escorts, a mine warfare force of 26, and about 24 coastal combatants, including several OSA missile boats.

The Soviet intelligence collector (AGI) GIDROFON observes the U.S. aircraft carrier CORAL SEA during a refueling operation. Soviet AGIs and surveying ships regularly monitor U.S. and NATO naval operations, and keep watch off several major bases, strategic straits, and other areas of military and maritime activity.

# NAVAL WEAPONS

The ADMG-630 Gatling-Action 6-Barrel 30-mm AA gun is replacing the older twin 30-mm on most Soviet Naval Combatants for close-in defense against ASCM.

The quad SS-N-14 antisubmarine missile launcher on a KRESTA II missile cruiser. This weapon carries a homing torpedo to a range of about 25nm.

The twin 57mm dual purpose gun of an ASW frigate. This is a fully automatic water-cooled gun system.

The twin SS-N-3 cruiser missile launcher on the KRESTA I missile cruiser. The launcher is hydraulic elevated to the firing position in this view.

The 152mm (6 inch) triple gun turrets on a SVERDLOV class cruiser. Although these ships are now approaching 30 years of age the Soviets still actively maintain them as flagships and shore bombardment platforms.

The SA-N-1 GOA missile launcher on a Soviet destroyer. The Soviets consider this a dual-purpose, antiship and antiaircraft weapon.

This six-barrel ASW rocket launcher is found in several classes of Soviet surface warships. Their range is several thousand meters.

Twin 76mm dual-purpose gun mounts, as in this KARA class cruiser, are fitted in several cruiser, destroyer, and frigate classes.

Twin 30mm rapid-fire guns, as shown here, and multi-barrel "Gatling" guns are fitted in Soviet ships for close-in defense.

The after section of a KARA-class missile cruiser shown here reveals the ship's ten torpedo tubes for ASW or antiship torpedoes, the SA-N-3 GOBLET missile launcher, and, alongside the hangar, RBU-1000 ASW rocket launchers.

# Section 5. Soviet Naval Personnel

*However technically perfect the Navy may be, man is always the basis of naval forces, the ruler of all the weapons of warfare.*

Admiral of the Fleet of the Soviet Union
S.G. GORSHKOV

The officers and men of the Soviet Navy occupy a respected position within Soviet society. Military service in the Soviet Union is characterized as a special form of service to the State and is rewarded by a continuous deluge of praise and commendation from Soviet public leaders and the press. The Navy is also given a special place of respect in Soviet eyes due to its close association with the revolution and connections with the Party, the 1921 Kronshradt rebellion notwithstanding. Finally, even more tantalizing to the average Soviet citizen, for whom travel to a distant foreign place is a virtual impossibility, is the opportunity which the navyman has to see the world in some of the most modern warships afloat.

The enlisted men are either two-year or three-year draftees; the latter term of service is required if the conscript is assigned sea duty. The Soviety Union does not draft women for military service. They are employed in clerical and support positions, and are not considered an integral part of the armed services as are service women of the United States.

Of approximately 443,000 uniformed personnel of the Soviet Navy, about 185,000 serve in ships and 59,000 are attached to naval aviation. In addition to the 12,000 man Naval Infantry force, another 8,000 are assigned to coastal defense activities, about 54,000 are engaged in various stages of training, and 125,000 are used to provide shore support. Additionally, a large number of civilians, perhaps as many as 30,000, form the crews of the majority of Soviet naval auxiliary ships.

## A. Pre-Service Training

The 1967 Law of Universal Military Service provides for draft eligibility at age 18 and naval service of three years (two years if serving ashore, a term which is comparable to that of the other armed services).

Pre-induction military training in the Soviet Union is under the control of the local military commission which organizes and administers the program. For those enrolled in the normal ten-year school program or a vocational technical school, military training is conducted in school during the 9th and 10th grades. Students who finish their education at the 8th grade level receive military training at their place of employment. This military training is a 140-hour program over a two-year period which includes military indoctrination, schooling in basic military skills, and weapons instruction.

In addition to compulsory training, paramilitary clubs and military specialist preparation courses are conducted by the DOSAAF (All-Union Voluntary Society for Assistance to the Army, Air Force, and Navy). DOSAAF clubs and specialist courses are frequently oriented toward a particular service. The more general clubs prepare the inductee for military service, usually in the army, while specific courses are designed to provide the specialized training that would otherwise be conducted while the conscript was in the service. Thus, there are Navy clubs which teach sailing and seamanship, as well as the more intensive and specific courses for radio operators, helmsmen, and divers. This training not only aids the military in reducing in-service instruction time, but also offers to Soviet youth opportunities to participate in activities which are denied to other members of Soviet society.

Taken at face value, these pre-draft and paramilitary programs appear quite formidable. On the other hand, the Soviet press periodically voices relatively strong criticism of their quality. Nevertheless, even a broad brush introduction to military training and the attendant physical exercise must ease the burden of military preparation. Further, some DOSAAF-trained specialists, usually in the less technically demanding disciplines can adequately fulfill their fleet assignments without further specialist training.

Upon completion of their active navy duty the conscripts, about 130,000 yearly, are retained on the reserve lists until they are 50 years of age. This provides a large pool of semi-trained manpower, especially those men who are only four or five years removed from their active service.

## B. Enlisted Men

The enlisted man of the Soviet Navy is a conscript with limited training and little career inclination. Conscripts are drawn from all the 16 republics within the U.S.S.R., and often those from Asian republics speak little Russian. Since conscripts are inducted into the services twice a year, this means that every six months about 15 percent of the naval enlisted strength is replaced by recruits.

### Basic Training

The new inductee undergoes a nine-week basic training program, after which he is either sent to a specialist school or directly to a duty assignment. A small number of recruits that have previously completed a DOSAAF specialty are sent directly to sea duty from basic training, while those judged physically or intellectually substandard are assigned to shore duty (as librarians, storekeepers, etc.). Approximately 75 percent of the men entering the Navy undergo specialist training, after which they receive their first shipboard assignment.

### Specialist Training

Soviet technical training is of four to six months' duration. Specialists graduate with an apparent understanding of the theoretical complexities of their own specialty but with little practical training. Consequently, the more significant and practical training for the enlisted man is received after he arrives on board ship.

Once aboard, the enlisted man will be assigned to a more senior sailor who, along with the officers and warrant officers in his department, will train him as his replacement. The new specialist then begins his study for a class specialist rating of Master 1, 2, or 3. If a sailor passes his Master 3 specialist test, fulfills certain requirements of the Party youth organization (Komsomol), and has no disciplinary violations, he will be rated "outstanding" by his ship's captain. The number and class of specialists and the number rated outstanding is considered a significant measure in evaluating a ship's perfor-

mance. It is not surprising, therefore, that over 90 percent of all seamen are rated Master 3 specialists by the end of their first tour of duty.

Rudimentary school instruction and limited time and facilities for intensive shipboard on-the-job training and testing leaves the Soviet specialist able to perform only the more routine functions of maintenance and general operation of a very limited range of equipment. To alleviate some of these shortcomings shipboard equipment is, for the most part, assembled from standard components and modules.

### Training At Sea

On board training is viewed as the major method of "perfecting skills and knowledge" to maintain a high level of combat readiness. Training at sea revolves around communist competition which entails the achievement of specified goals and objectives set by the commanding officer and political officer in conjunction with the staff. Some objectives and goals are prescribed in terms of the number of men achieving a new or higher class specialization and the number of men rated as outstanding.

Competitive drills and exercises are conducted aboard ship. These involve the usual variety of situations from damage control to simulated or actual firing of weapons. Fleet and inter-fleet exercises involve units competing against each other. All competition is characterized by the great emphasis that is placed upon obtaining set quantitative goals. This has resulted in a number of abuses. Aside from outright cheating, other abuses involve the setting of unrealistically low goals which are easily achieved, or the more serious problem of "formalism" in which, after the goals are set, promises made to fulfill them, all the required speeches made, then the whole competition is just forgotten. A further problem involves drills and exercises which are conducted in a routine, mechanical manner, thereby lacking realism and constructive value.

Obviously, the true extent to which these problems exist in Soviet training cannot be determined. Yet, if the reports of the Soviet press can be considered an indication, it would appear that such problems are not rare in Soviet training.

### Shipboard Life

On his first tour of service the Soviet draftee receives low pay, even by Soviet standards (3.8 rubles per month—4.8 if on sea duty—which at the official exchange rate equals $6.50/mo.), and leave totaling only up to 20 days over a three year period. During this term of service he is under close supervision and

Figure 7

| HIGHER NAVAL SCHOOLS (5-YEAR PROGRAMS) | | |
|---|---|---|
| School | Location | Specialization |
| Frunze Higher Naval School | Leningrad | Line |
| Makarov Pacific Ocean Higher Naval School | Vladivostok | Line |
| Kirov Red Banner Caspian Sea Higher Naval School | Baku | Line |
| Kaliningrad Higher Naval School | Kaliningrad | Line |
| Nakhimov Black Sea Higher Naval School | Sevastopol | Line |
| Leninskiy Komsomol Higher Naval School of Submarine Navigation | Leningrad | Submarine-line |
| Dzerahinskiy Order of Lenin Higher Naval Engineering School | Leningrad | Line-engineering |
| Sevastopol Higher Naval Engineering School | Sevastopol | Line-engineering |
| Popov Higher Naval Communications School | Leningrad Petrodvorets | Radio-electronics |
| Lenin Higher Naval Engineering School | Pushkin | Shore engineering |
| Kiev Higher Naval Political School | Kiev | Politics |

| POSTGRADUATE COURSES | | |
|---|---|---|
| Order of Lenin and Ushakov Naval Academy Imeni Marshal of the Soviet Union A. A. Grechko | Leningrad | Advanced technical and staff education (equivalent to U.S. Naval War College) |
| Naval Officers Technical School | Kronshtadt | Officer technical training |
| Higher Naval Courses | Leningrad | Officer technical training |
| Higher Military Academy of the General Staff (All Services) | Moscow | General staff training |

subject to continuous political indoctrination. Sea duty can best be described as rigorous. Distant deployments often include long periods in open-water anchorages, and the infrequent liberty runs ashore in foreign ports are normally done in supervised groups during daylight hours. Living conditions aboard the modern classes of Soviet ships is, by Western standards, spartan but acceptable, whereas conditions aboard older classes, such as the PETYA and KOTLIN, are cramped and rather trying. Viewed in the relative terms of the standard of civilian housing in which many naval recruits previously lived, their shipboard accommodations are probably more than adequate.

# C. Warrant Officers

The Soviet Navy faces a chronic shortage of senior enlisted personnel. The reenlistment rate averages under 10 percent, in part because of the national requirement that all males must serve on active duty in the Soviet armed forces. In an effort to overcome the aforementioned shortage, and to upgrade the status of a career serviceman the rank of warrant officer (Michman) was instituted in 1971. At completion of compulsory service the Soviet sailor, if considered capable, is offered additional specialist and military training in a two-year warrant officer school in return for a five-year reenlistment, including schooling.

**Figure 8**
**COMPARISON OF SOVIET AND U.S. NAVAL GRADES AND RANKS**
**OFFICER GRADES**

| Rank* | Approximate U.S. Equivalent |
|---|---|
| Admiral of the Fleet of the Soviet Union | Fleet Admiral |
| Admiral of the Fleet | Admiral |
| Admiral | Vice Admiral |
| Vice Admiral | Rear Admiral |
| Rear Admiral | Commodore Admiral |
| Captain 1st Rank | Captain |
| Captain 2nd Rank | Commander |
| Captain 3rd Rank | Lieutenant Commander |
| Captain Lieutenant | Lieutenant |
| Senior Lieutenant | Lieutenant (junior grade) |
| Lieutenant | Ensign |
| Junior Lieutenant | Ensign |

**WARRANT GRADES**

| | |
|---|---|
| Warrant Officer (Michman) | Chief Warrant Officer |
| | Warrant Officer |

**NON-COMMISSIONED RANKS**

| | |
|---|---|
| Chief Ship's Petty Officer | Master Chief Petty Officer |
| | Senior Chief Petty Officer |
| Chief Petty Officer | Chief Petty Officer |
| Petty Officer First Class | Petty Officer First Class |
| Petty Officer Second Class | Petty Officer Second Class |
| Petty Officer Third Class | Petty Officer Third Class |
| Senior Seaman | Seaman |
| Seaman | Seaman Appretice/Recruit |

*Naval aviation, naval infantry, and coastal defense personnel, although an integral part of the Navy, have "military" ranks, such as general, major, and sergeant.

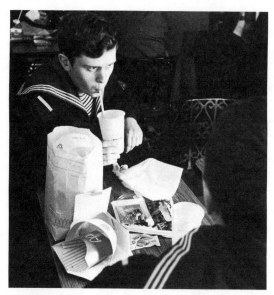

Two Soviet sailors enjoy a "taste" of capitalism with a "hamburg and fries" during the Soviet Navy visit to Boston in commemoration of "VE" (Victory in Europe) day.

The warrant officer is designated the principal interface between officers and enlisted men. In this capacity he is given more responsibilities than a senior petty officer and, as a result of his more extensive training and experience, he can relieve the officers of some of the more technical duties which the conscript is not qualified to perform. Benefits increase considerably as pay, privileges, and leave offered to the warrant officer approach that of an officer. In addition, he is also offered the opportunity to achieve promotion to officer ranks after a number of years of service.

# D. Officers

The regular sea-going Soviet naval officer, a career man, is a volunteer who has been carefully selected, well trained, and highly specialized. He is more often than not a relative of a Party official or another naval officer and ethnically, a Great Russian.

## Schooling

The large majority of regular naval officers are now drawn from specialized naval schools. A small number begin as reserves after graduation from civilian universities and a few others win promotion from the warrant officer ranks. A youth normally starts his career as a cadet at one of 11 higher naval schools after a vigorous selection program. The course of study is intense and lasts five years, with the graduates receiving a National Engineering Diploma and the rank of lieutenant. Some Soviet officers begin their naval careers at about age 15 upon entering the Nakhimov naval school system for young men, and then going into a higher naval educational institution upon graduation from the Nakhimov school.

The higher naval schools can be divided into two types: line and engineering. Six line schools graduate officers as specialists in one of three areas: navigation, weapons, and antisubmarine warfare, which correspond to three of the five to seven departments of a Soviet warship. Graduates from one of three other higher naval engineering schools and one radio electronics school are assigned to ship radio electronics and engineering departments. There is also a higher naval school for shore duty engineering specialists and one which trains political officers for service with the fleet. Other naval specialist officers such as medical, legal, and finance are trained in higher schools with their army counterparts. Naval aviation officers receive their basic flight training with the Air Forces.

## Early Career

Upon graduation, a regular officer is assigned to a ship for duty in the department which corresponds to his specialty (navigation, engineering, ASW, etc.). The new officer usually spends the first three to six years of his career in the same department aboard the same ship or at least in the same class of ship. During this period the new officer earns a classification as a specialist in his technical pursuit. He must pass the examinations to stand watch and for certification as a supervisor as he progresses through positions equivalent to assistant division officer, division officer, assistant department head, to department head.

## Responsibilities

In the Soviet Navy the officer is both the manager of his unit and the major technical specialist. He is expected to be able to do virtually everything his subordinates can do, as well as to instruct them in their duties, and to care for their "ideological well being." Because of the general low level of technical competence of his enlisted men, the Soviet officer tends, in some cases, literally "to do everything," even the most routine maintenance. A Soviet junior officer's duties as manager, technician, instructor, and loyal Party member give him quite a heavy work load. Complaints are frequent, yet, in spite of these, the typical Soviet officer appears to fulfill his duties adequately.

### Command

The selection of a commanding officer is a highly subjective process based on the principle that the commanding officer of a ship should select and train his own replacement. During the early years of an officer's service, his CO evaluates his performance and eligibility for command. As a vacancy occurs the ship's captain appoints the officer of his choice as executive officer and organizes and supervises a program of study for his development. During this period of study the line officer matures from a narrow specialist to a broad generalist capable of command. Upon successful completion of the demanding command-at-sea test, the officer succeeds the CO in command of the ship, or is assigned to command another ship of the same or a similar class. The length of time in an officer's first command varies with the individual and the ship, but averages between three to five years.

Those not considered qualified for command and those in the engineering categories, who, by virtue of their specialty, are not considered for command, become career specialists. Officers in these fields continue to receive promotions while serving as department heads and on staffs afloat or ashore.

## E. Senior Officers

Considerable emphasis is placed on post-graduate education, and after command at sea an advanced

A Soviet rear admiral and his staff discuss mutual interests with a U.S. rear admiral during the visit of two Soviet destroyers to Boston. Soviet naval officers tend to be more specialized than their U.S. counterparts, with a major effort being undertaken to broaden their education as they approach selection for flag rank.

Soviet sailors, several with cameras, prepare to go ashore as their guided missile destroyer visits Massawa, Ethiopia. Although Soviet Navy life is spartan by American standards, modern Soviet warships are relatively comfortable and naval service provides these young men with travel and technical training opportunities not available to most of their countrymen.

degree is considered a prerequisite for posts of higher responsibility and flag rank. Officers with an average of six to eight years of experience, usually after their first command, take graduate training at the Grechko Naval Academy, an institution roughly equivalent to the U.S. Naval War College, or other schools offering advanced degrees. As an alternative to study in residence at a higher naval school, an officer can obtain an advanced degree by correspondence, requiring only limited residence.

After graduate work, the senior line officer generally serves on the staff of a group of ships of the same class that he commanded. Later, he rotates between fleets and other related tours are assigned to develop broader experience. Further, either immediately before or after promotion to flag rank, he will usually attend the joint service academy for general staff officers.

For those officers in "career specialties" the logical assignment after graduate training is to a position on the faculty of one of the naval schools or to

a tour in one of the technical directorates (such as shipbuilding, mines, or torpedoes), as he proceeds toward flag-rank position in his area of expertise.

From the brief discussion above several major deficiencies may be clearly discerned in the education and experience of the Soviet naval officer. He spends the first part of his career as a specialist in a very narrow field, restricted to one department in one class of ship. As a result, the junior officer lacks needed broad experience and versatility. Often it is only upon selection as executive officer that he begins to develop the broader experience necessary for more senior posts. Because of the strong emphasis on collective thinking and Party-enforced discipline, the junior officer is often seriously lacking in personal initiative, original thinking, and the willingness to take responsibility; leadership characteristics that are necessary for command. But for those chosen to move up the promotion ladder, the positions held, education received, and training taken from midcareer onward imply that an officer finally selected

**Figure 9**
**SOVIET NAVY HIGH COMMAND**

for flag rank is both educated and experienced.

The base pay for Soviet officers initially appears nominal, but taken in combination with the total allowances and benefits which accrue to a military officer in the Soviet Union, the real income is substantial. For example, naval officers are given significant additional pay for service in northern areas, for service in submarines and aircraft, for sea duty, and for command. Military officers are a prestigious and privileged class in the Soviet Union and receive extensive benefits, according to rank, well beyond those of the average citizen.

## F. Leadership

The highest office in the Soviet Navy is that of Commander-in-Chief (CINC). The position, currently held by Admiral of the Fleet of the Soviet Union Sergei G. Gorshkov, carries with it responsibilities for the operation and administration of the Soviet Navy. In addition, as head of one of the five military services, he serves as a Deputy Minister of Defense, a political position, which in the United States is filled by the Secretary of the Navy. Thus, Gorshkov simultaneously holds positions which in the U.S. would be equal to Chief of Naval Operations and Secretary of the Navy. Directly below the CINC is the First Deputy Commander-in-Chief, Admiral of the Fleet N.I. Smirnov, who is the assistant to the

CINC in the operational direction of the fleet.

At the next level are eight Deputy CINCs responsible for several different administrative, technical, logistical, and training functions. Additionally, there is a Navy Staff composed of the heads of several directorates which serves the CINC in policy and planning. Below this level are the fleet commanders. Each fleet is headed by a flag officer, with the fleet organizational structure quite similar to that of the CINC of the Soviet Navy.

Soviet flag rank officers tend to remain in their posts longer than their U.S. counterparts, with Admiral Gorshkov an exceptional case in point. His naval career spans 55 years of which almost 25 have been spent as CINC of the Soviet Navy. Most senior officers of the Navy serve long tours in their respective posts. However, there have been several changes at naval headquarters in Moscow during the past few years, which might provide a hint to Admiral Gorshkov's successor. The front runners presently appear to be Fleet Admirals Yegorov and Smirnov, Chief of Main Naval Staff and First Deputy CINC, respectively.

Admirals in senior positions are generally in their late fifties and early sixties. A signficant aspect of the Soviet philosophy toward high-level positions is that long term assignments and specialization do not necessarily destroy flexibility or effectiveness in leadership.

Figure 10
FLEET ORGANIZATION

## G. Political Activity

All sectors of the Soviet military are subject to political indoctrination and close Communist Party monitoring which is even more extensive than in the civilian sector. Of course, a higher percentage of Soviet naval officers are Party members than in the civilian population. The stress upon political reliability is all-encompassing and of foremost importance. This stems from the concern of the Party to maintain a military force that is completely subordinate, thereby rendering it incapable of exercising military power for its own political ends.

Americans generally have difficulty differentiating between the Soviet State and the Communist Party, and hence the relationship of the Navy to the Party. The difficulty is, that for all intents and purposes, the State and the Party are indivisible. Their key leaders are virtually the same and their goals are identical. In essence, the Politburo of the Central Committee of the Communist Party is the ruling body of the U.S.S.R. with the "state" organization primarily running the day-to-day business of the nation. Several members of the Politburo also serve on the Presidium of the Supreme Soviet (or Congress), with the Presidium being the highest state body.

Over 90 percent of all naval officers are members of the Party or the Komsomol (Young Communist League). It is a rare officer who has not learned that demonstrating one's political activity is essential to a successful career. Further, Party membership is essential to obtain command. The Party, with representatives at all echelons of command within the armed forces, is headed in the Navy by a four-star admiral. Each ship has a political officer (Zampolit) who has his own separate chain of command. His duties aboard ship are diverse: he directs the ideological indoctrination and monitors the political reliability of the officers and men; directs "socialist" competition; ensures that Party decisions are carried out; enforces discipline; and acts as both "chaplain" and social worker for the crew to promote morale.

The nature of Party control sets up groups within the command structure; the CO and line officers comprise one part, and the political officer and the party organizations the other. Problems and tension are sometimes created between groups as they perform their functions. On one hand, an officer's military authority can be undermined since, as a member of the Party, he is as susceptible to party criticism and discipline as any other Party member. On the other hand, the Zampolit, while wearing the uniform of a naval officer, was in the past clearly not nautically qualified and, in many cases, was looked down upon by the professional naval officers. In recent years, however, there has been a trend toward giving the political officer practical naval experience as a line officer prior to his entry into the political field.

There is a significant commonality of interest between the Zampolit and the professional officers since both share responsibility for the successful operations of a ship and its performance in the "socialist" competition by which their careers are judged.

The Soviet thrust to the sea extends beyond warships. This photograph shows the passenger liner RUSSIA and a commercial hydrofoil at the Black Sea port of Odessa. The Soviet Union operates more passenger ships and more commercial hydrofoils than any other nation.

# Section 6. Other Soviet Maritime Activities

*". . .Among the main components which we included in the concept of the sea power of the state are the state's capabilities to study (investigate) the ocean and exploit its resources, the condition of the transport and fishing fleet and its ability to support the needs of the state, and also the presence of a navy adapted to the interests of that state, since antagonistic social systems are present in the world. . ."*

*Admiral of the Fleet of the Soviet Union*
*S.G. GORSHKOV*

The extensive and intensive use of the sea by the Soviet Union over the last two decades has not been limited to naval operations. In the best traditions of Mahan, the Soviets have embraced the whole spectrum of activities which are considered part of the Sea Power "equation"—merchant marine, fishing, oceanographic research, shipbuilding, a large pool of experienced seamen, and a knowledgeable leadership.

The Soviet concept of sea power encompasses constant and coordinated use of all aspects of its natural, scientific, industrial, merchant, and naval resources in support of state policy. All the various elements of Soviet maritime activity have been developed by the deliberate allocation of resources as a matter of prime importance to the Soviet Union.

## A. Merchant Marine

The application of the Soviet basic philosophy of sea power is clearly demonstrated in the ongoing development of the Merchant Marine. At the end of World War II the Soviet oceangoing merchant fleet consisted of about 400 ships totaling approximately two million deadweight tons. The ships were relatively small, old, and slow. In fact, the newest and best were the lend-lease "Liberty" ships that the United State had provided the Soviets during World War II.

In just over three decades, the Soviet oceangoing merchant fleet has emerged from an insignificant, coastal oriented flotilla to rank fifth in the world in numbers of ships, and ninth in terms of deadweight (carrying) tonnage. The expansion continues. Today the Soviet Union has an oceangoing merchant fleet of nearly 1,720 ships aggregating over 18.6 million deadweight tons. By comparison, the U.S.

Merchant Marine, with just over 580 ships equalling approximately 19.5 million deadweight tons, ranks eleventh in number of ships and eighth in carrying capacity. However, the U.S. Merchant fleet is largely composed of large tankers and non-self-sustaining container ships, units which would be less advantageous to us in time of crisis.

The Soviet merchant fleet is presently operating on over 70 different international trade routes, calling at over 125 countries throughout the world. Prior to the boycott by U.S. longshoremen, a result of the Afghan invasion, Soviet merchant ships were calling at nearly 60 different ports along the U.S. East, West, and Gulf coasts as well as in the Great Lakes.

The growth of the Soviet Merchant Marine has paralleled a period of equally dramatic world-wide maritime development, but the Soviet accomplishments have been unique. While the international growth has been spurred by the demand for big oil tankers, bulk carriers and container ships, the Soviet Union has carefully directed the growth of its merchant fleet, not allowing purely commercial pressures of modern trade to dictate its composition. It is of interest to note that while most nations have reduced their passenger-carrying fleets, the Soviets continue to expand theirs and today have the largest passenger fleet in the world.

As a result, the Soviets today possess one of the few major merchant fleets which can perform either a peacetime commercial mission or satisfy military logistics requirements effectively and efficiently should a conflict arise. This has been achieved by accepting some economic disadvantages in exchange for functional versatility. Rather than building only supertankers, container ships, liquid gas tankers and bulk carriers, the Soviets have improved the designs of their large, sophisticated cargo ships and small, multi-purpose tankers. They also have stressed the building of high-speed, Roll-On/Roll-Off (RO/RO) combination vehicle and container ships. The RO/RO ships offer the Soviets considerable versatility.

The RO/RO ship is basically a floating garage that loads and unloads cargo via a large ramp, so it can easily transport most forms of military hardware without ship modification. Moreover, it does not need sophisticated port facilities. The Soviet Union has more than 40 RO/RO ships operational and other numerous specialized ships are scheduled to be delivered in the near future. These ships can operate on the most competitive commercial routes, yet they can be, and have been, reallocated with very little delay to serve as military sealift or logistics ships.

The Soviets have recently received two large, SEABEE barge transport ships (U.S. design) from Finland. The SEABEE represents another advanced concept in cargo handling; it can transport large unit loads, such as 1,300-ton barges, and has the potential for use in military logistics or amphibious lift operations. Cargo is loaded with a stern-mounted, 2,700-ton-capacity elevator. Up to 25,000 tons of cargo can be off-loaded in only 13 hours. A SEABEE ship could contribute significantly to Soviet military operations.

The Soviet 1976–1980 five-year plan calls for a growth in foreign trade of 30 to 35 percent, with particular emphasis on expansion of commerce with the capitalist world. In addition, the Soviet Union intends to use its merchant fleet to carry its own trade. Available figures indicate that the Soviet Merchant Marine transports approximately 60 percent of its own imports. (By comparison, the U.S. Merchant Marine carries less than five percent.)

The five-year plan also projects a cargo carrying capacity increase of over 4 million deadweight tons. If the net gain stated in their goal is reached, the Soviet oceangoing merchant fleet will consist of approximately 1,800 ships totaling nearly 19.5 million deadweight tons by 1981. All indications are that the following five-year plan will also see a 4 million deadweight ton growth.

The Soviet Merchant Marine has proved to be an effective tool for the extension of Soviet influence, as well as an instrument for neutralizing or eliminating free world influence in strategic areas. Past activities of the merchant fleet in support of Soviet State policy, especially in African, Middle Eastern, and Indian Ocean waters, are contributing to a growing political acceptance of the Soviet presence in these areas.

The Merchant Marine, on a regular basis, provides a significant amount of the logistics support required by the Soviet Navy, particularly to those ships operating in waters distant from the U.S.S.R. This gives the Soviet Navy a high degree of flexibility in the employment of its forces. Additionally, these merchant ships have a much greater freedom of access to the ports of the world than do navy ships or auxiliaries and thus can purchase fresh water, produce and other supplies for naval use in

A Soviet roll-on/roll-off (RO/RO) ship lowers her 60-ton capacity stern ramp to take aboard vehicles.

ports where warship visits might be denied.

Today, Soviet merchant ships operate on all oceans, calling at ports throughout the globe. If a Soviet ship is in distress in distant waters, it usually is only a matter of hours before other Soviet ships arrive at the scene to assist.

In summary, Soviet leaders, no doubt, see the Merchant Marine providing the following advantages and capabilities:

• a large national resource providing valuable hard-currency income, services, and employment;

• an instrument to provide support for the foreign policy of the state and to further the cause of Soviet Communism;

• a source of much needed foreign currency in a continuing "balance of payments" battle;

• a visible sign to the world of the prestige and power of the Soviet Union;

• a training system for an expanding pool of trained seamen;

• a closely coordinated logistics force for meeting the needs of the Soviet Navy on a regular basis.

• a world-wide network of intelligence collection; and

• a highly organized, closely controlled organization which can provide military support quickly and effectively, particularly for amphibious operations or arms movements.

Overall, the Soviet Union is expected to continue to develop a multi-mission Merchant Marine which can compete economically in international markets and provide many other services in support of State policy, while maintaining the ability to respond rapidly to any need for extensive military support. Thus, the merchant fleet provides the U.S.S.R. with a growing capability for the world-wide support of political, military, and economic influence.

## B. Fishing

The Soviet Union operates the world's largest fishing fleet with nearly 4,000 ocean-going vessels. The fleet's catch in 1975 exceeded 10 million tons. This catch placed the Soviets second behind Japan, and was more than three times the size of the U.S. catch.

Considerable resources have been invested in the fishing industry in the postwar period, with emphasis on the construction of large, high-capacity ocean-going ships equipped with elaborate fish-finding devices and processing facilities.

The Soviets exploit fishing grounds throughout the world's oceans with large flotillas of ships. Groups of 100 to 200 trawlers are not unusual and, on occasion, much larger formations have been reported. Trawlers which can handle up to 50 tons of fish per day often are equipped to filet, salt, can or freeze the catch on board. Large factory ships and refrigerated cargo ships also receive processed and unprocessed fish from the smaller trawlers. The factory ships have the necessary processing and

The sleek-looking passenger liner MAKSIM GORKIY at a Far Eastern port. The Soviets use many of their passenger ships in the lucrative vacation cruise trade to earn hard Western currency. The Soviets have approximately 70 large passenger ships in service.

ELEVATOR IN LOWERED POSITION

storage facilities aboard and can transfer their fish products at sea to cargo ships which take them to market. There is little waste—that part of the catch which is not processed into food is usually turned into fish meal or fertilizer without delay.

These fishing flotillas are usually self-contained "communities," supported by specialized repair ships, tugs, tankers, and fresh water vessels. On occasion these auxiliary ships also support naval activities. When a Soviet HOTEL class ballistic missile

This port-quarter stern view of the Soviet merchant ship INZEHENER MACHULSKIY shows the ship's stern ramp in the raised position. She is a roll-on/roll-off vehicle-carrying ship with space for coontainers or vehicles on her main deck. The Soviet merchant marine is large, modern, and flexible.

submarine encountered engineering difficulties in the North Atlantic in 1972 the submarine was assisted for several days by support ships for the fishing fleet.

Soviet fishermen are among the highest paid workers in the U.S.S.R. They are compensated for the hardships of long voyages and climatic extremes with annual paid vacations often exceeding two months. The industry also is a major employer of Soviet naval reservists.

Most fish caught by the Soviet Union (over 90 percent) is for human consumption and eaten by the Soviet people or given as aid to Soviet client states. It has been estimated that 20 percent of the Soviet protein consumption consists of seafood. Exports include such delicacies as caviar, squid, and king crab. The latter is caught in great quantities off the coast of Alaska, and has been the subject of a continuing controversy as well as given rise to several treaties between the United States and the Soviet Union.

The Soviet's large whaling fleet has also brought it (and that of the Japanese) into a running conflict with world conservationists who are seeking to save a number of whale species from extinction.

Since the Soviet fishing flotillas "invaded" U.S. coastal fishing grounds in 1961, there has been much debate on Soviet "vacuum cleaner" fishing methods and the damage done to the U.S. fishing industry. The establishment in 1977 of a 200-mile economic zone around the United States has placed limits on catch and strict control of fishing activities on foreign fishing ships within the zone. Masters of several Soviet fishing vessels have been placed under arrest by the U.S. Coast Guard for violating these controls. The Soviets are now faced with a large number of such economic zones established by countries with contiguous traditional fishing grounds.

The "universality" of fishing has led to considerable export of Soviet fishing equipment and technology to other countries. Similarly the Soviet Union has purchased a large number of fishing units from East German, Poland, and other nations.

**The Soviet merchant ship BALASHIKHA is pushed to a pier by harbor tugs at Nantes, France. In addition to servicing the long Soviet coastlines, the Soviet merchant fleet carries on an active and profitable trade with the West and the Third World.**

The massive Soviet fishing fleet has its own training and research ships, the latter including the EKVATOR shown here. For several years two converted WHISKEY-class submarines were employed in the fisheries/oceanographic research role. They have been discarded.

It is likely that there will be a continuing growth in the quality of the fishing industry and in the size of its fishing fleet as well. There are indications that in the not too distant future, the Soviets will be the undisputed world leader in this area of maritime endeavor, which is increasing in importance as the earth's population grows and seeks additional animal protein.

## C. Research and Surveying

Soviet maritime activity is supported by the world's largest fleet of ocean-going research and surveying ships, totaling over 200 ships. These ships are separate from the naval intelligence ships (AGI) discussed in Section 4. Rather, they are engaged in academic and economic studies and operational research of the oceans. A number of these ships are Navy subordinated and manned by Navy crews, but the majority belongs to civilian institutes concerned with ocean research and are civilian manned. Obviously, the civilian segments of research activities have close ties with those of the Soviet Navy and, again, the officers of the civilian manned ships include a number of naval reservists. In addition, the

A Soviet "fish factory" ship operates with part of her brood of smaller fishing craft off Cape Cod in the Western Atlantic. These large ships are floating bases and can completely process and can a catch on board. The Soviet Union has more than 4,000 ocean-going fishing craft and support ships, plus numerous inshore fishing boats, all directed by a centralized ministry.

The Soviet satellite tracking ship KOSMONAUT YURI GAGARIN is one of a fleet of Soviet Space Events Support Ships (SESS) which are employed in civilian and military space and missile programs. The large, sophisticated ships of this type have secondary intelligence collection and political presence capabilities. Most of these ships are operated by civilian research institutes, with a few others being Navy manned.

Soviet Union operates a large number of Space Event Support Ships (designated SESS) that provide worldwide spacecraft and satellite tracking and recovery capabilities. This extensive use of SESS units is in marked contrast with the U.S. policy of primarily placing space tracking stations ashore around the world.

Activities of the research, surveying, and space support ships are managed by the several institutes of the Academy of Sciences of the U.S.S.R. that direct scientific research. These institutes maintain close coordination with both the Navy and the Main Fisheries Administration, with the latter organization operating several research ships. During the 1960s two modified Navy submarines also were used for fishing research and in the 1970s several naval submarines were employed on oceanographic research expeditions.

Soviet research ships are generally of modern design with most being of Finnish, Polish or East German construction. These ships vary in size from small coastal craft to the giant KOSMONAUT YURI GAGARIN, a 45,000 ton ship fitted with elaborate equipment for research into the upper atmosphere and support of space events.

## D. Shipbuilding

The current Soviet shipbuilding industry evolved after World War II when the devastated yards of the Baltic and Black Sea coasts were rebuilt. Additionally, new yards were constructed (or enlarged) on the Northern and Pacific coasts to make those naval fleets more independent of the traditional European yards.

Today the Soviet Union has 18 large shipyards, each employing 2,000 or more workers on a full-time basis. It is not, therefore, unreasonable to state that the U.S.S.R. ranks as one of the world's largest producers of ships. However, because of the Soviet emphasis on small merchant ships and fishing craft, the Soviet tonnage production is small for the number of ships produced.

Besides receiving the output of a large indigenous ship-building industry, the Soviets also purchase a considerable amount of merchant and naval tonnage from foreign yards. Naval ships, particularly amphibious ships and auxiliaries are purchased from Poland, Finland, and East German as are merchant and fishing ships from the aforementioned countries plus others, including France, Japan, West Germany, Sweden, and Great Britain.

Soviet submarines are built at Severodvinsk on the White Sea, the largest submarine building complex in the world; at Komsomolsk, well up the Amur River near the Pacific coast; at Gorkiy, which is in the center of the U.S.S.R., with ships moving to the open sea via the extensive Soviet inland waterway system; and, at the two-yard United Admiralty complex in Leningrad. It is estimated that these yards have capacities great enough to produce 20 to 25 nuclear submarines a year on a single-shift basis, if priority was given to allocating necessary resources and labor from other sources. The Soviets have been building about 8 to 10 new submarines annually, most nuclear powered, over the last several years.

Principal surface combatants are, for the most part, built in Leningrad and Kaliningrad on the Baltic Sea, and Nikolayev near the Black Sea where the KIEV class carriers are now being built. A number of other yards are involved in the construction of lesser combatants and other types of naval ships.

Most of the shipyards which build warships also build merchant or fishing ships. The construction of all ships, naval or commercial, in the Soviet Union is managed by the Ministry of Shipbuilding. This ministry is responsible for all yards of significant size; for most research, design, and useful exchange of technologies; and for a coordinated allocation of resources. Each aspect of ship design, construction, and specialized equipment is supported by a specialized research institute.

New shipbuilding equipment, from a simple hand tool to a computer-controlled cutting machine, must be approved by the Ministry of Shipbuilding before it is introduced as a standard item. Similarly, techniques initially employed for merchant construction (such as modular assembly of components on a floating platform) subsequently are applied to naval shipbuilding.

The KOSMONAUT VLADIMIR KOMAROV is also a Soviet Space Events Support Ship (SESS) named in honor of a deceased astronaut. The ship's radar antennas are enclosed in plastic spheres; the horn-like antennas on the masts are for satellite communications.

The oceanographic research ship AKADEMIK SASHKIRIYA, shown here underway in the South China Sea, is a modern AGOR built in East Germany for Soviet service. The civilian-manned ship is typical of the large Soviet ocean research fleet that supports military and civil activities.

The Soviet yards make extensive use of modern shipbuilding techniques and technologies. According to a U.S. Navy report on the subject: "In formulating a judgment on U.S.S.R. progress in automation of (ship) production . . . most of the publicized innovations are related to yards doing merchant work of a far more open nature and considerably lower priority than Soviet naval work, and it can therefore be presumed that in yards engaged in high priority work on naval ships, the facilities, equipment, and technology are at least equal and probably superior. . ." Various Soviet shipbuilding management and production techniques that have been observed have led to the conclusion that the Soviets have established a very strong and viable shipbuilding industry.

In addition to building naval and commercial ships for Soviet use, Soviet shipyards have produced ships of both categories for other nations in the Warsaw Pact, Western Europe, and the Third World.

# Section 7. Key Questions

## 1. Which Navy is the larger?

In terms of the ships the U.S. Navy is clearly outnumbered by the Soviet Navy, by a ratio of 3 to 1. Although we dominate in aircraft carriers, the Soviet Navy has 80 more principal surface combatants, 235 more submarines, six times as many auxiliaries, and a large land-based aviation strike force. Amphibious ships of the U.S. Navy are much larger and more capable, but this is a warfare area where the Soviets have greatly increased their capability over the last decade. Furthermore, the quality of their naval forces is steadily improving, though it is still not equal to the quality of our own. The U.S. Navy clearly has a large advantage in sea-based aircraft and a greater number of uniformed personnel.

In contrast to Soviet Navy forces, those of the U.S. Navy have declined substantially since the late 1960's. These reductions have restricted our flexibility in fulfilling peacetime commitments worldwide, and limited our offensive options in many critical and high threat areas in time of war. A strategy of sequential offensive campaigns based on a careful alignment of our objectives in order of relative importance is required for the U.S. to succeed in gaining effective control of those sea areas essential to our successful prosecution of a global war.

The table overleaf depicts the trends in the size of U.S. and U.S.S.R. naval forces, and illustrates the marked decline in the size of the U.S. Navy since 1969. By comparison, Soviet reductions have been modest and primarily involve the retirement of smaller coastal defense ships.

## 2. Which Navy is the stronger?

Simple numerical comparisons are but one measure for drawing conclusions about the strengths of navies. In the nuclear-electronic-missile age the "equation" has become most complicated. Also,

the U.S. and Soviet Navies have been built differently for different missions. The power potential of each, but more particularly the Soviet Navy, is related to the distance its naval forces operate from its homeland. Thus, the Soviets can bring much more weight of arms to bear close to the Soviet littoral than they can in mid-Atlantic or mid-Pacific. In some functions the Soviet Navy is the stronger, while in others the U.S. Navy excels.

The U.S. Navy is generally considered to lead in the areas of:

    Carrier Aviation
    Amphibious Assault
    Submarine Detection
    Submarine Noise Level Control
    Underway Replenishment
    Nuclear Surface Ships

The Soviet Navy is generally considered to lead in:

    Antiship Missiles
    Number of Submarines
    Small Combat Craft
    Ocean Surveillance
    New Technology Application
    Shipbuilding Capacity and Initiative
    Mine Warfare
    Integration of Maritime Resources
    Numbers of Conventional Surface Ships
    Command and Control Structure

With respect to a comparison of U.S. and Soviet Navies, Admiral Gorshkov has observed that:

*The qualitative transformations which have taken place in naval forces have also changed the approach to evaluating the relative might of navies and their combat groupings: we have had to cease comparing the number of warships of one type or another and their*

---

viet naval BEAR D maritime surveillance aircraft approaches a U.S. aircraft carrier in the Pacific. Just off the R's starboard wing is an F-4 PHANTOM fighter from the carrier. These mid-ocean intercepts of U.S. ships by Soviet aft are apparently for intelligence collection and flight crew training. The BEAR first entered service with Soviet -Range Aviation in 1956.

total displacement (or the number of guns in a salvo or the weight of this salvo), and turn to a more complex but also more correct appraisal of the striking and defensive power of ships, based on a mathematical analysis of their capabilities and qualitative characteristics.

### 3. Should NATO navies be countered in U.S.-Soviet comparisons?

Most definitely, and the navies of the Soviet's Warsaw Pact allies should also be counted in these types of net comparisons. If the U.S. and the Soviet Navy should ever go to war it would most likely be a NATO/Warsaw Pact conflict. The contributions of the NATO navies to the Alliance are considerable.

Strategically, Britain and France each operate a small force of nuclear powered ballistic missile submarines. Britain, Canada and France have significant naval forces and maritime commitments beyond European waters. Yet most NATO naval forces are designed to operate in the littoral waters of Europe supporting NATO's flanks and keeping the vital sea lanes open. Therefore, other NATO navies concentrate in coastal defense, antisubmarine and mine warfare tasks, with NATO assignments, for the most part, in waters proximate to their homelands. U.S. naval forces seldom operate in the Baltic and Black Seas where the great bulk of maritime defense rests on the NATO countries whose shores are washed by those seas.

It must be remembered, however, that the second most powerful force in the Soviet Navy is the Pacific Ocean Fleet which, except for its naval air element, is too far removed from the NATO area of responsibility to be an immediate threat. But that fleet is of prime concern to the U.S. and our Pacific allies, for one must accept that a NATO/Warsaw Pact war could not be confined to the European area. Therefore, the Soviet Pacific threat can not be divorced from that in Europe.

### 4. Why have the Soviets waited so long to build aircraft carriers?

Since the dramatic changes in Soviet government and policies of the mid-1950s the Soviet Navy has not always attempted to compete where the U.S. Navy is strongest. Rather, the Soviets have developed other forces and weapons to counter the U.S. Navy, such as submarines and antiship missiles. Initially it would have been very difficult for them to compete in an areas of naval warfare such as carrier aviation with the same type of assets. The United States already had several decades of experi-

Figure II.
## NAVAL COMBATANT FORCE LEVEL TRENDS

| | 1969 US/USSR | | 1979 US/USSR | |
|---|---|---|---|---|
| **ACTIVE FLEET** | | | | |
| **Warship Classification** | | | | |
| Aircraft Carrier Type | 22 | 0 | 13 | 2 |
| Surface Combatant Type | 279 | 220 | 178 | 269 |
| Submarine Type | 156 | 354 | 123 | 357 |
| Command Type | 2 | 0 | 0 | 0 |
| **Other Combatant Ship Classification** | | | | |
| Patrol Combatant Type | 9 | 148 | 3 | 120 |
| Amphibious Warfare Type | 153 | 103 | 63 | 91 |
| Mine Warfare Type | 74 | 165 | 3 | 165 |
| **Auxiliary Ship Classification** | | | | |
| Mobile Logistics Type | 112 | 56 | 59 | 150 |
| Support Type | 119 | 624 | 20 | 610 |
| **TOTAL ACTIVE FLEET** | 926 | 1670 | 462 | 1764 |
| **NAVAL RESERVE FORCE\*** | | | | |
| **Warship Classification** | | | | |
| Surface Combatant Type | 35 | ** | 20 | ** |
| Submarine Type | 20 | ** | 0 | ** |
| **Other Combatant Ship Classification** | | | | |
| Patrol Combatant Type | 6 | ** | 0 | ** |
| Amphibious Warfare Type | 1 | ** | 3 | ** |
| Mine Warfare Type | 14 | ** | 22 | ** |
| **Auxiliary Ship Classification** | | | | |
| Mobile Logistics Type Support | 0 | ** | 2 | ** |
| Support Type | 1 | ** | 6 | ** |
| **TOTAL NAVRESFORCE** | 77 | ** | 53 | ** |
| **NAVAL FLEET AUXILIARY FORCE** | | | | |
| **Auxiliary Ship Classification** | | | | |
| Mobile Logistics Type | 0 | *** | 12 | *** |
| Support Type | 4 | *** | 13 | *** |
| **TOTAL NAVFLTAUXFORCE** | 4 | *** | 25 | *** |
| **TOTAL SHIP OPERATING FORCE** | 1007 | ** | 540 | ** |

\*Ships of the Naval Reserve Force are in commission and not in "mothballs." This chart does not include those ships in either the U.S. or Soviet navies which are "inactive."

\*\*Not available.

\*\*\*A daily average of 6 Soviet merchant ships, from a total fleet of over 1,700 ships, routinely support Soviet naval out of area operations.

ence as well as an existing force of supercarriers along with their highly specialized aircraft.

Also significant is the fact that one of the prime

missions of the U.S. Navy in time of war includes the projection of power overseas to support allies and protect broad ocean areas. The aircraft carrier is a key factor in the "projection" and "sea control" missions. Soviet "projection" forces to date have been primarily either politico-economic in concept, ground military forces, or naval surface ships. Other priorities had to be met in the Soviet order before the large endeavor of aircraft development could be undertaken.

Construction of the KIEV class carriers, however, now demonstrates that the time has arrived for aircraft carrier-type ships to be added to the Soviet Navy. Along with the Soviet development of amphibious forces, the Soviet Navy will greatly improve its ability to meet sea control and projection objectives with the addition of the KIEVs, the expected larger carrier of the eighties, the new warship classes under construction, and the expanding merchant marine. Some observers see the carrier and the aforementioned programs as the instruments with which the Soviets plan, for the first time, to challenge U.S. Naval supremacy on the high seas beyond the waters which the Soviets currently view as critical to their defense.

## 5. How experienced is the Soviet Navy?

The Soviet Navy had minimal open ocean combat experience in World War II and none since that war. By comparison, some senior officers of the U.S. Navy saw extensive combat during World War II, and others in the Navy as a whole have had con-siderable combat experience in certain combat disciplines during the Korean and Vietnam wars. Also, U.S. naval personnel have had considerably more ocean-going experience during the three decades since World War II. However, the Soviets are rapidly expanding their pool of trained seafarers in the Navy as well as in the merchant and fishing fleets. Their ability to operate ships and aircraft over the oceans of the world at great distances from the Soviet Union has increased steadily.

## 6. Are aircraft carriers vulnerable to Soviet Missiles?

Soviet air, surface, and submarine-launched guided or cruise missiles are the primary military threat to all surface warships. However, the aircraft carrier is probably the least vulnerable and most survivable because of its extensive damage-control features and the inherent defensive capabilities of its embarked air wing. The aircraft carrier is essentially a mobile airbase, giving it greater flexibility and subject to less political sensitivity than a fixed base. Also in certain other aspects a carrier is less vulnerable—it can maneuvered to minimize risk, is not subject to political denial, and is not susceptible to guerilla attack.

The modern U.S. aircraft carrier is thus considered highly survivable in comparison with other general purpose forces, and at the same time, is recognized (particularly by the Soviets) as one of the most powerful and versatile weapon systems ever developed.

# Appendix A. STATEMENTS BY LEADERS WITHIN THE DEPARTMENT OF DEFENSE CONCERNING THE EXPANSION OF SOVIET SEAPOWER

*The following comments on the maritime balance between the United States and the Soviet Union are extracted from the "Defense Department Annual Report for Fiscal Year 1981" by Secretary of Defense Harold Brown (29 January 1980):*

In 1979, the Soviet military effort was about 50 percent larger than our own, measured by what it would cost to buy Soviet progams (including personnel) in the U.S. economy. We now estimate that the Soviets are using somewhere between 11 and 14 percent of their Gross National Product for defense purposes, compared with out five percent (of a U.S. GNP nearly twice as large).

The difference between Soviet and U.S. investments in military goods (R&D, procurement, and military construction) is even larger. In the past decade, Soviet investment has been cumulatively about 27 percent larger than ours. In 1979 alone, it was probably greater by 85 percent. The consequences of that investment are now becoming evident.

In strategic nuclear forces, the Soviets have come from a position of substantial numerical inferiority 15 years ago to one of parity today—and a potential for strategic advantage if we fail to respond with adequate programs of our own. Their forces have improved in quality as well as in numbers. They have deployed two new generations of ICBMs and SLBMs, and are working on a further generation— each generation being of increased sophistication and capability.

Some components of the increasingly modern Soviet Navy are intended for the direct defense of the U.S.S.R. Other parts are designed for antisubmarine warfare and the interdiction of the major sea lanes. Still other parts are clearly intended for the long-range projection of Soviet military power. The Soviets have consistently sought to use air and naval facilities overseas, and they have expanded their capability for long-range sealift and airlift as well. There has been recent evidence that they intend to use their airborne divisions for power projection— in the Arab-Israeli October war of 1973 and in Afghanistan in 1979–80 . . . .

. . . with the appearance of the BACKFIRE bomber in increasing numbers, Soviet naval aviation could come to be a bigger threat to our sea lines of communication and naval forces than Soviet submarines. Although we have AEGIS ships under construction to counter this growing threat, we still lack sufficient defenses against massed missile and bomber attacks on convoys and battle groups.

## Naval Forces

While the overall size of the Soviet general purpose naval forces has not changed significantly since last year, we observe in their construction programs ships that appear to reflect a change in the mission orientation of the Soviet Navy. The ocean-going surface warship force consists of two KIEV class light, VSTOL, guided missile carriers already in service (with a third carrier fitting out); two MOSKVA class guided missile aviation cruisers, and 269 other surface warships, including 19 with antiship missile launchers. A nuclear-powered warship described in 1979 continues fitting out in Leningrad, and could be in service by 1981. A sister ship is under construction, and three other new classes of smaller cruisers displacing from about 7,600 to 12,000 tons are being built.

SVERDLOV class cruiser, ALEKSANDR SUVOROV, "with a bone in her teeth" steams in the Philippine Sea during the Exercise EAN. Although over 25 years old the Soviets still utilize these old "work horses" extensively.

Construction also continues of KRIVAK II and GRISHA class frigates. We estimate that the Soviets deliver ocean-going surface warships at a rate of about 10 a year.

The Soviet active general purpose submarine force (excluding SSBNs and SSBs) consists of 270 boats. Of this total, 205 are attack submarines, 65 are cruise missile submarines, and several are auxiliary diesels. Some of the cruise missile boats can launch antiship missiles while submerged. Current general purpose submarine construction is now running at a rate of about 10 boats a year.

The Soviets assign around 370 of their medium bombers to Naval Aviation, including a considerable number of BACKFIREs. The majority of these aircraft, supported by the Soviet system for ocean surveillance, will be able to attack ships with air-to-surface missiles at extended distances from their home bases. . . .

The Soviets now deploy a total of 91 amphibious warfare ships, of which 26 are capable of open-ocean transit and exended operations. The new 13,000 ton IVAN ROGOV class Amphibious Assault Tranport Dock (LPD) was assigned to the Pacific Fleet last year. It is designed to operate high-speed air-cushion landing craft. The Soviet merchant marine also has the capability to support overseas operations, especially with roll-on/roll-of ships, of

which 45 are now in service. The Soviet naval infantry force consists of about 12,000 men.

Direct support of Soviet naval forces comes from 85 underway replenishment ships. There are also 65 material support ships and 135 fleet support ships providing direct underway support to Soviet naval forces. The introduction of the 40,000 ton fleet oiler (AOR), BEREZINA, means that Soviet ships are no longer confined to anchorages for refueling. It is expected that more of these modern logistics ships will enter the Soviet fleet in the 1980s. In addition, the first Soviet hospital ship reportedly was launched in Poland early in 1979. Soviet writings indicate that there is a need for large, high-speed hospital ships to give close support to combat fleets in distant waters.

## Distant Operations

As part of the evolution of their general purpose forces, the Soviets have been taking a number of steps to improve their capability for operations increasingly distant from their borders.

Their roll-on/roll-off (RO/RO) ships are ideal for transporting and rapidly loading and unloading wheeled and tracked vehicles, even in less developed harbors. The Soviets, in fact, made extensive use of

A BORIS CHILIKEN class replenishment oiler refuels a KYNDA class missile cruiser underway with two span wires supporting five refueling hoses.

their RO/RO ships to resupply Ethiopia in her conflict with Somalia.

The KIEV class carriers, with their vertical take-off and landing (VTOL) FORGER aircraft, HORMONE helicopters, long-range antiship missiles, and ASW weapons, could engage in limited power projection missions. They have the capability to provide escort for Soviet sealift operations and a measure of air support for amphibious assaults. Perhaps more important, they can make the risk of outside interference with these activities look high. We are already observing on increased Soviet naval presence in such distant areas as the Indian Ocean, and their newly-acquired access to Vietnamese air and naval facilities is being used with increasing regularity. The large and sustainable new cruisers that will become operational in the next few years will give the Soviets additional capability to project power at great distances from their own homeland.

much greater dependence on sea lines of communication. Soviet naval forces would be hampered in time of war because of geographical restrictions on easy access to open seas and sustainability limitations, but their current primary mission of sea denial and interdiction is less demanding than NATO's mission of sea control.

## Projecting Power to Areas Remote from the Soviet Union

Soviet efforts to create a capability for distant power projection involve both the development of new types of military forces and the careful manipulation of a wide range of indirect methods of intervention. There are many indications that the Soviets have embarked on a serious, long-term program to develop forces to provide a major capability for

*The following excerpts are from the statement by the Chairman of the Joint Chiefs of Staff General David Jones, USAF, presented to Congress in January 1980 on "United States Military Posture for Fiscal Year 1981";*

## Balance in the Atlantic and Other Maritime Areas

At sea, as on land, the military balance is shifting against NATO. While U.S. and allied naval forces decline in number, the Soviet Union is developing a total naval force whose size and quality combine to threaten NATO's ability to carry out its maritime strategy. This multi-dimensional threat appears even in peacetime in a wide range of maritime activities ranging from passive intelligence collection to increasing Soviet operations on both flanks of Europe and in other strategic areas of the world.

Although some comparisons favor the United States and NATO, the overall trends are adverse. Soviet increases in strength and capability are not balanced by countervailing NATO measures. The numbers of Soviet ships and submarines have not changed greatly, but improvements in endurance, armament, and amphibious and ASW capabilities are being achieved as new and more versatile ships enter the Soviet naval inventory. Soviet cruise missiles are a particularly dangerous threat to U.S. and NATO forces, especially when complemented by Soviet land-based naval and long-range aviation. The growth of Soviet and Warsaw Pact naval capabilities is especially disturbing in light of NATO's

power projection. They now have the means to deploy small, lightly equipped combat forces to distant locations. Such forces could be expected to cope successfully with the kind of disorganized and militarily weak opposition which they are likely to encounter in many regions of the Third World. The Soviets have introduced a new class of large amphibious assault ships to expand their sealift. The first two ships of a new class of vertical/short take-off and landing aircraft carriers are now at sea; larger carriers may appear in the future . . . the lack of tactical air capability at a distance is a serious Soviet deficiency. U.S. naval forces are generally superior to Soviet forces, although the margin is diminishing as the Soviets expand and modernize their "blue water" fleet. Soviet naval forces are hampered by poor sustainability at long distances from port and by greater vulnerability to air and submarine attack.

The following has been taken from "A Report by Chief of Naval Operations, Admiral Thomas B. Hayward, U.S. Navy, on the Fiscal Year 1981 Military Posture and Fiscal Year 1981 Budget of the United States Navy" presented to the House Armed Services Committee in January 1980:

. . . Given the narrowness of our margin of superiority today, every major engagement must be regarded as potentially decisive in terms of its impact on the naval balance. With our numerically inferior forces, achievement of favorable attrition ratios offers the only prospect of progressively defeating the Soviet Navy in a worldwide war at sea. A one-for-one exchange ratio is a sure formula for defeat. . . . last year I testifed in some detail about the size and characteristics of the Soviet Navy, so I will not dwell on comparisons of ship numbers and tonnages, which may not be the most relevant criteria for consideration. Rather, I would prefer to highlight some of the insights we have gained over the past twelve months into the direction in which the Soviets are going, and the pace and momentum of their naval improvement program. The fact is, they are building large, sophisticated and highly capable new ships which give us a clear vision of the Soviet Navy of the '80s, and offer reenforcing evidence of their determination to achieve maritime superiority within the decade.

We are now seeing on the high seas, on a routine basis, the results of major policy and investment decisions made by the Soviets five to eight years ago. With the appearance of each new class of ship and aircraft, the Soviets have improved their operating radius, their staying power, and their war-fighting capability. Many of the Soviet developments foreshadowed in my posture statement last year have since been translated into a full-fledged operational capability. Two KIEV class aircraft carriers now operate with the Soviet fleet. The second of these, the MINSK, was transferred last summer to the Pacific Fleet, underlining the Soviet's intention to challenge our control in all the sea areas of strategic importance. The Russians' sea-based air capability does not yet come close to matching our own; but it is evident that the KIEVs are simply a stepping stone to a more elaborate and versatile carrier capability. After the remaining ships of that class now under construction have joined the fleet, I would expect them to be followed by a new, larger class of carrier, probably nuclear powered.

To keep the significance of the Soviet carriers in perspective, one must remember that they represent an *addition* to the large land-based naval air force which the Soviets have always possessed, whose strike air regiments have about the same number of attack aircraft that we have in our twelve carrier air wings. Those regiments are being modernized by the addition of the long-range, supersonic, BACKFIRE aircraft, which will comprise the majority of the force by the latter half of the 1980's. The marriage of BACKFIRE with modern long-range, air-launched cruise missiles makes the BACKFIRE a quantum improvement in Soviet naval aviation, and represents a major increase in the threat to military and commercial shipping of the United States and its allies. So the notion that the Soviets have lagged in the application of airpower to warfare at sea is totally erroneous. They have always accorded it high priority; and, with the addition of aircraft carriers to their existing large land-based naval air force, they are acquiring the capability to use air power even more flexibly, and at greater distances from the U.S.S.R.

In the surface combatant area, four new classes of cruisers are now under construction. One of them, which we believe to be named the KIROV, is nuclear powered and over twice the size of our latest class CGN. More properly termed a battle cruiser, it is heavily armed with new generations of surface-to-surface and surface-to-air missiles. This is a spectacularly impressive warship, which should attract wide attention when it first puts to sea later this year.

This past year saw the Russians commence extended operations of the world's deepest diving, fastest, and only titanium-hulled submarine, the ALFA class. The Soviets continue to impress us with their submarine building capacity—currently the world's largest, and still growing—now producing five classes with the potential for an expanded construction rate in future years.

Other new Soviet ship types which made their first distant deployment in 1979 give important clues to the direction of Soviet intentions. The 40,000 ton BEREZINA replenishment ship is as good as our best, and will provide an improved capability for sustained operations by Soviet battle groups anywhere in the world. The 13,000 ton Soviet amphibious ship IVAN ROGOV—like the MINSK, recently transferred to the Soviet Pacific Fleet—provides the Russians with an improved amphibious assault capability as sophisticated as anything we have, in a well-designed multi-purpose hull. Additional ships of both classes are expected.

During the past year the Soviets have made further progress in expanding their access to overseas support facilities. Their ships and naval aircraft are frequently seen at ports and airfields in Vietnam. Their use of Aden airfields for Indian Ocean reconnaissance flights have reached new levels and Soviet advisers continue overseeing the expansion of naval facilities in Cuba, which we must assume would be available to the Russians in a crisis.

In summary, there has been no slackening in the Soviet Union's determination to build a large, high-quality navy that is capable of challenging us worldwide. Where once they were building 1,200 ton PETYA escorts for coastal defense, they are now constructing a wide variety of large, open-ocean, offensively capable cruisers, carriers, logistic support ships, amphibious assault ships and submarines. We would be naive and foolhardy not to expect them to continue to expand on this capability in the years ahead.

- Destruction of enemy naval forces, especially submarines and aircraft carrier task forces—sea denial;
- Protection of ocean areas for Soviet military and economic use—sea control;
- Strategic nuclear strike and deterrence;
- Support of ground forces, primarily in areas contiguous to the Soviet Union;
- Cutting of enemy sea lanes;
- Support of Soviet foreign policy in all areas of the world; and
- Projecting power ashore, that is, naval and air bombardments and landing troops even in areas remote from the Soviet Union.

The increasing Soviet capability to carry out these missions puts an entirely new perspective on the naval threat, and its direct effect on U.S. national interests. From the beginning of our country, American strength and well being has been predicated on control of the seas by naval forces friendly to the

*The following are portions of the statement by the Director of Naval Intelligence, Rear Admiral Sumner Shapiro, U.S. Navy, on the Soviet naval threat today:*

The close of the 1970s is more than a convenient benchmark for the Soviet Navy; it is in fact a significant milestone which marks the end of a full generation of dramatic Soviet naval progress and accomplishment. It has brought within grasp a Russian aspiration nearly three centuries old: an open-ocean navy capable of actually influencing world events. The signs are clear and unmistakable: there has been a major shift in the basic mission of the Soviet Navy, and as a result, the new Soviet leadership in the 1980s will have at their disposal political and military options never before available to them. The implications of this development to the U.S. and our allies are worrisome, to say the least.

The Soviet Navy of today and the foreseeable future is the dream of Admiral of the Fleet of the Soviet Union, Sergei Gorshkov, for nearly 25 years its commander-in-chief and architect. He has savored that rare pleasure in history of planning and then seeing through to completion a massive and successful national undertaking.

Already established as the greatest Russian naval builder since Peter the Great, Gorshkov at age 70 probably has at least a few more years to consolidate and expand what he has termed the "balanced fleet." Balanced to Gorshkov means being capable of achieving any or all of the broad range of traditional naval missions:

United States. Since World War II, America itself has virtually had a monopoly on naval strength. This has allowed us great latitude in conducting our foreign policy and promoting world peace.

Work toward ending that monopoly began in earnest shortly after the Soviet humiliation in the Cuban missile crisis, in which the overwhelmingly powerful general-purpose navy of the U.S. was decisive. Even while closing the strategic nuclear gap, the Soviets began 15 years ago to redress this naval imbalance and establish conventional naval forces that could support Soviet interests worldwide.

In 1964, Soviet warships began what has become a continual presence in the Mediterranean. In 1968, they moved into the Indian Ocean. In 1969, they began periodic deployments in the Caribbean. In 1970, the Soviet Navy expanded operations off the Western coast of Africa. Overall, their operations away from their home waters have increased eight-fold since 1965.

It is significant that during the same period, the Soviet Navy figures prominently in such international crises as the 1967 and 1973 Arab-Israeli Wars, the Bangladesh War of 1971, the Cuban intervention in the Angolan civil war in 1975, and the Somalia-Ethiopian war of 1977. Soviet warships appeared off of Vietnam last year to demonstrate their support of the Vietnamese against China. Soviet

A PETYA class small frigate shows the effect of long deployments and a poor paint job. The previous side number "852" shows through the blistering paint. The Soviets often reassign side numbers when ships deploy. This is more a function of fleet precedence than a deception device as crews can sometimes be seen over the side painting new numbers while transiting through international straits.

ships have continued to visit the Vietnamese ports of Danang and Cam Ranh Bay every since. As in other areas where the Soviets have established a naval presence, Vietnam is also being used periodically as a staging base for Soviet Navy long-range maritime surveillance aircraft.

And everybody is well aware of the role that the Soviet Navy is playing in the Indian Ocean during the current crisis.

During this critical generation of Soviet naval development, top priority was obviously given to matching the U.S. nuclear submarine missile force. In the last 10 years, the Soviets have built about 55 nuclear ballistic missile submarines . . . And although the rate of construction has leveled off, we expect the Soviets to continue building even larger ballistic missile submarines, with long range, more accurate missiles.

Even while building this nuclear deterrent force, the Soviets have succeeded in developing a formidable and increasingly capable number of general purpose submarines. They can attack enemy sub-

marines, surface ships, and coastal targets with conventional or nuclear weapons, both torpedoes and cruise missiles which are launched while submerged. The Soviets added about eight submarines in 1979. A majority of these were nuclear attack types, bringing the total of general purpose nuclear submarines built to date to almost 100.

The emergence of the strong surface naval challenge has been the most dramatic Soviet military development of the 1970s. They have significantly increased the number and quality of large multi-mission, high-endurance, missile-equipped principal surface combatants.

Over the past 10 years, the Soviets have built an average of 12 principal surface combatants each year. Nine were delivered in 1979 alone.

Their largest is the KIEV, the Soviet's first aircraft carrier. Its operational appearance in 1976 represented the initiation of sea-based tactical aviation in the Soviet Navy, forecasting the day when the Soviets might cut the tether of land-based air support. The second of its class, the MINSK, joined the fleet in 1978. The third was launched that same year and is being fitted out for operations; probably beginning in 1981.

The Soviet Navy's entry into the aircraft carrier picture has received a lot of attention, as well it might. And we will be watching closely to see what comes next in the way of seaborne tactical air. But in some respects, even more ominous for the 1980s is the recent beginning of four new classes of even larger, more powerful, more sophisticated cruisers being built rapidly in Soviet shipyards. Over 10 are now being built; the first several should be operational in the next several years, and it is conservatively estimated that about 25 could be completed by the end of the 1980s. They will be armed with new weaponry, including a long-range antiship cruise missile system, two antiaircraft missile systems, and a dual-purpose gun for use against other ships and shore targets.

Of great interest to us is the fact that one of these classes will be nuclear powered. It is the Soviet's first nuclear-powered surface combatant and the largest noncarrier combatant built by any nation since WWII. The first of this class is expected to be operational this year, and a second is under construction.

Further evidence of Soviet naval ambition is found in the new emphasis on larger, more capable amphibious ships. This is on top of a modest force of 25 LSTs built in the 1970s, numerous smaller amphibious ships, and an increasing number of merchant ships readily adaptable to amphibious support.

The centerpiece of the growing force, the IVAN ROGOV, debuted in 1978 and operated extensively in 1979. At 13,000 tons, three times the size of their next largest amphibious warfare ship, the ROGOV is designed to carry about 550 troops with their equipment, and put them ashore not only with conventional landing craft, but by helicopters and air-cushioned vehicles as well.

Soviet naval aviation made great strides during this past generation also. Its most recent advances have been introduction of the KIEV class carriers that can launch fixed-wing aircraft at sea, the advent of the BACKFIRE supersonic, missile-armed bomber, and continued deployment of TU-142 ASW aircraft.

As the Soviets enter the 1980s there is increasing evidence that the KIEV class carrier with its VTOL aircraft is but a stepping stone in the Soviet program to develop a seaborne tactical air capability approaching that of the U.S. Although not conclusive, the accumulated evidence points to the development of a larger conventional take off and landing (CTOL) aircraft carrier by the end of the decade. If, indeed, the Soviets continue this progression, a new carrier would probably be nuclear-powered.

What I have just reviewed for you is the Navy the Soviets have today. It is impressive. What is more impressive, however, and of longer range significance is the capital investment the Soviets have made in their shipbuilding industry—both surface and submarine construction yards. Five shipyards are building submarines, eight are building surface warships, and several others produce minor warships and auxiliaries. Of the 13 principal shipyards, almost all have undergone a major modernization and extensive expansion in the last five years. Capital investments of this magnitude are not made unless there are long range plans for continued major naval construction programs. The yards now available to the Soviets are capable of easily sustaining construction rates far in excess of the rates we have seen during the past decade.

The sum of these efforts is impressive. A generation ago a defensive coastal force, outclassed by several other navies, the Soviet Navy in 1980 is second only to us and this trend of increasing capabilities continues into the foreseeable future.

1980 is the last year of the current Soviet five-year plan. For the world to see, the Soviets will probably have failed to reach many goals, especially in their domestic economy. But also for the world to see is a naval building effort which, by any measure, has been a success.

1980 is also the end of a generation of Soviet naval achievements. It is likewise the beginning of a new naval age, both for the Soviet Union and the United States, as the two navies grow more evenly matched in an open-ocean competition that alters the course of history.

In summary, the thought I would like to leave with you is that there are clear and unmistakable signs that the Soviet Navy is changing its orientation and its mission. Defense of the Homeland is still paramount in Soviet strategic planning, and the Soviet Navy figures prominently in such plans. However, the balanced fleet which Admiral Gorshkov conceived and built has far greater capabilities than are required for a purely defensive role. The Soviet leadership obviously recognized the increased political and military options that such a navy affords them. They have proved this, both by the way they employ their Navy in support of Soviet national interests today, and by the mammoth capital investment and resource commitment they are making in their Navy's future.

**BEAR D maritime surveillance/reconnaissance aircraft.**

# Appendix B. SOVIET NAVY ORDER OF BATTLE
## (December 1980)

## 1. Active Ships

### Submarines—Nuclear Powered

| | | |
|---|---|---|
| *SSBN | Ballistic Missile Submarines (YANKEE, DELTA classes).... | 62 |
| SSBN | Ballistic Missile Submarines (HOTEL class) .............. | 8 |
| *SSGN | Cruise Missile Submarines ..... | 50 |
| *SSN | Torpedo-Attack Submarines ... | 55 |

### Submarines—Diesel-electric Powered

| | | |
|---|---|---|
| SSB | Ballistic Missile Submarines .... | 17 |
| SSG | Cruise Missile Submarines ..... | 20 |
| *SS | Torpedo-Attack Submarines ... | 160 |

### Aircraft Carriers and Helicopter Cruisers

| | | |
|---|---|---|
| CVHG | VSTOL Carriers (KIEV class) ................. | 2 |
| CHG | Helicopter Cruisers (MOSKVA class) ............. | 2 |

### Cruisers

| | | |
|---|---|---|
| *CGN | Guided Missile Cruiser (Nuclear) (KIROV class) .............. | 1 |
| *CG | Guided Missile Cruisers (SAM/SSM**) ............... | 25 |
| CL | Light Cruisers (SVERDLOV class) ........... | 9 |

### Destroyers

| | | |
|---|---|---|
| DDG | Guided Missile Destroyers (SAM/SSM**) ............... | 36 |
| DD | Destroyers .................. | 30 |

### Frigates (Escorts)

| | | |
|---|---|---|
| *FFG | Guided Missile Frigates (KRIVAK class) .............. | 28 |
| *FF/FFL | Frigates/small frigates ......... | 140 |

### Small Combatants

| | |
|---|---|
| *Missile Craft ........................ | 145 |
| *Patrol/ASW/Torpedo Craft ............ | 395 |
| *Minesweepers (Fleet, Coastal, Inshore) ... | 400 |

### Amphibious Ships

| | | |
|---|---|---|
| *LPD | Amphibious Assault Transport Dock (IVAN ROGOV class) .... | 1 |
| LST | Amphibious Vehicle Landing Ships (ALLIGATOR, ROPUCHA classes)..................... | 25 |
| LSM | Medium Landing Ships (POLNOCNY/MP-4 classes) ... | 60 |

### Auxiliary Ships

| | |
|---|---|
| *Mobile Logistics Ships ................ | 150 |
| *Other Auxiliaries Ships ................ | 610 |

---

*Indicates additional units under construction in these categories.

**All Armed with Surface-to-Air Missiles (SAM); some additionally armed with Surface-to-Surface Missiles (SSM).

***Numbers are approximate in many instances. It is noted that "Small Combatants" and "Auxiliary Ship" categories include a large number of craft which would not be "commissioned" ships in the U.S. Navy.

## 2. Active Aircraft
### (including helicopters)

Strike/Bombers ......................... 370

    BACKFIRE
    BADGER
    BLINDER

Fighter/Fighter Bombers .................. 90

    FITTER
    FORGER

Reconnaissance/Electronic Warfare Aircraft . 170

    BADGER
    BEAR D
    BLINDER

Antisubmarine Aircraft.................... 390

    BEAR F      HOUND
    HAZE       MAIL
    HORMONE  MAY

Tanker Aircraft ......................... 70

    BADGER

Transport/Training Aircraft ............... 340

Total approximately 1,430

## 3. Personnel Strength

| | |
|---|---:|
| Afloat................................. | 185,000 |
| Naval Aviation ....................... | 59,000 |
| Coastal Defense ..................... | 8,000 |
| Naval Infantry ...................... | 12,000 |
| Training ............................. | 54,000 |
| Shore Support ....................... | 125,000 |
| Total | 443,000 |

# Appendix C. SOVIET WARSHIP DESCRIPTIONS

*Our Navy is a focal point for the most recent achievements of science and technology. Nuclear missiles, powerful propulsion plants, and radar and electronic equipment have given it new qualities and advanced the Navy into the rank of forces of strategic significance.*

Fleet Admiral N.I. SMIRNOV
First Deputy Commander-in-Chief
Soviet Navy

This appendix provides basic descriptive data and photographs of the more significant Soviet submarines and surface ships.

Arrangements: Submarine classes are arranged alphabetically, followed by surface combatants arranged generally by size and lastly the amphibious ships.

Classification: The dimensions, characteristics, and general information are approximate.

Designations: Simplified ship designations have been used in this appendix; they are not necessarily the formal designations assigned by U.S./NATO navies. All ships' class names are NATO code names except those indicated by asterisks, which are transliterations of the actual Soviet names.

The Soviets do not necessarily classify their ships as we do in the West. Following are a sampling of the transliterations from Russian of Soviet ships types, with their English meanings and the classes so identified:

BDK —BOL'SHOY DESANTNYY KORABL' = Large Landing Ship (IVAN ROGOV, ALLIGATOR)

BPK —BOL'SHOY PROTIVOLODOCHNYY KORABL' = Large Antisubmarine Ship (KARA, KRESTA II)

EM —ESAKDRENNYY MINONOSETS = Fleet Destroyer Ship (KOTLIN)

MPK—MALYY PROTIVOLODOCHNYY KORABL' = Small Antisubmarine Ship (GRISHA, MIRKA)

PKR —PROTIVOLODOCHNYY KREYSER = Antisubmarine Cruiser (MOSKVA)

PLA —PODVODNAYA LODKA ATOMNAYA = Submarine, Nuclear (VICTOR, NOVEMBER)

RKR —RAKETNYY KREYSER = Missile Cruiser (KYNDA, KRESTA I)

SK —STOROZHEVOY KORABL' = Escort Ship (KRIVAK)

is foredeck view of the new nuclear powered missile cruiser, KIROV, reveals the high density of weapons carried. From t to right can be seen the circular "manhole" covers of the SA-N-4 missile launchers on the 02 level, the 20 large hatch as for the launchers of a new type antiship cruise missile; the 12 smaller covers for the new vertical launch surface-to-missile system (each of which probably covers a separate magazine loaded with a number of missiles); at the extreme ht of the picture can be seen the end caps of the twin SS-N-14 ASW missile launcher which is served by a multimissile gazine forward of it; lastly, 4 of the 8 30mm-Gatling guns can be seen on the deck houses either size of the large missile ches.

# SUBMARINES

**ALFA attack submarine**

## Nuclear Powered Attack Submarine (SSN): ALFA class

| | |
|---|---|
| Displacement: | 2,600 tons surfaced |
| Length: | 80 meters (262 feet) |
| Propulsion: | Nuclear |
| Main Armament: | torpedoes, probably ASW missiles |

The ALFA class SSN is the latest in the line of Soviet nuclear powered attack submarines. The hull, made of light-weight, non-magnetic titanium, is the most streamlined hull shape ever produced by the Soviets, suggesting that this submarine was designed to maximize speed, which is estimated to be over 40 knots. This is a small, high technology submarine with a very deep diving ability and probably is fitted with advanced weapons. The Soviets have been pursuing this program for a number of years and have several units of the ALFA class.

**BRAVO training submarine**

## Training Submarine (SST): BRAVO class

| | |
|---|---|
| Displacement: | 2,400 tons surfaced |
| Length: | 73 meters (240 feet) |
| Propulsion: | Diesel-electric |
| Main Armament: | torpedo tubes possible |

The BRAVO class SSTs entered the Soviet Navy in the late 1960s as target and training submarines. Only four units were produced. Although they are not viewed primarily as "attack" submarines, they may be armed with torpedoes.

## Nuclear Powered Cruise Missile Submarine (SSGN): CHARLIE I class

| | |
|---|---|
| Displacement: | 4,000 tons surfaced |
| Length: | 95 meters (311 feet) |
| Propulsion: | Nuclear |
| Main Armament: | 8 SS-N-7 antiship missiles |
| | torpedo tubes |

The first unit of this class became operational in 1968. Their SS-N-7 submarine launched antiship cruise missiles have a range of more than 55 kilometers (30 nautical miles). About twelve CHARLIE I SSGNs were built before being succeeded by the improved CHARLIE II program. Another cruise missile submarine program, the PAPA class, is somewhat larger than the CHARLIE, but there is little evidence that the Soviets have continued building this class beyond the initial unit.

**PAPA Class Submarine**

**CHARLIE II cruise missile submarine**

## Nuclear Powered Cruise Missile Submarine (SSGN): CHARLIE II class

| | |
|---|---|
| Displacement: | 4,300 tons surfaced |
| Length: | 103 meters (338 feet) |
| Propulsion: | Nuclear |
| Main Armament: | 8 SS-N-7 or SS-N-9 \antiship missiles |
| | torpedo tubes |

This is an improved CHARLIE II class SSGN. The larger size may accommodate an increased weapons and sensors capability. If the SS-N-9 is carried, it would improve this submarine's missile capability, including an extension of range to probably twice that of the 30 mile range of the SS-N-7.

**DELTA I ballistic missile submarine**

## Nuclear Powered Ballistic Missile Submarine (SSBN): DELTA I class

| | |
|---|---|
| Displacement: | 9,000 tons surfaced |
| Length: | 140 meters (460 feet) |
| Propulsion: | Nuclear |
| Main Armament: | 12 SS-N-8 strategic SLBMs |
| | torpedo tubes |

The DELTA class SSBNs are follow-on submarines to the YANKEE class. The first DELTA I went to sea in 1971. This SSBN carries 12 SS-N-8 SLBMs with a range of more than 7,500 kilometers (4,000 nautical miles). These missiles allow Soviet DELTAs to remain in range of most North American targets while in home waters.

**DELTA II ballistic missile submarine**

## Nuclear Powered Ballistic Missile Submarine (SSBN): DELTA II class

| | |
|---|---|
| Displacement: | 10,000 tons surfaced |
| Length: | 155 meters (508 feet) |
| Propulsion: | Nuclear |
| Main Armament: | 16 SS-N-8 strategic SLBMs |
| | torpedo tubes |

The DELTA II class, a lengthened version of the DELTA I, was first deployed in the Soviet Northern Fleet in early 1976. Other than its greater length and larger missile battery, the DELTA II is similar to the DELTA I SSBN.

**DELTA III ballistic missile submarine**

## Nuclear Powered Ballistic Missile Submarine (SSBN): DELTA III class

| | |
|---|---|
| Displacement: | 10,500 tons surfaced |
| Length: | 155 meters (508 feet) |
| Propulsion: | Nuclear |
| Main Armament: | 16 SS-N-18 strategic SLBMs |
| | torpedo tubes |

The DELTA III SSBNs are a follow-on to the DELTA II, and are similar in most respects, except for their more advanced, MIRV capable SS-N-18 missile. This weapon has a range of approximately 5,000 nautical miles. The missile compartment is higher in the DELTA III than in the DELTA II to accommodate the longer SS-N-18.

ECHO attack submarine

## Nuclear Powered Attack Submarine (SSN): ECHO class

| | |
|---|---|
| Displacement: | 4,500 tons surfaced |
| Length: | 110 meters (360 feet) |
| Propulsion: | Nuclear |
| Main Armament: | torpedo tubes |

Five ECHO I class cruise missile submarines (SSGN) were built from 1960 to 1962. These submarines were originally armed with six tubes for the SS-N-3 SHADDOCK cruise missile plus torpedo tubes. All five units have now been converted to an attack configuration (SSN) by removal of the missile tubes. Torpedoes now comprise their weapons capability. As SSNs, this class is known simply as ECHO without the suffix "I." It was a submarine of this class which had an internal accident off Okinawa in August 1980. A number of her crew were killed or injured; the submarine had to be towed to Vladivostok.

ECHO II cruise missile submarine

## Nuclear Powered Cruise Missile Submarine (SSGN): ECHO II class

| | |
|---|---|
| Displacement: | 5,000 tons surfaced |
| Length: | 115 meters (377 feet) |
| Propulsion: | Nuclear |
| Main Armament: | 8 SS-N-3/12 antiship cruise missiles |
| | torpedo tubes |

Twenty-nine ECHO II class SSGNs were completed between 1962 and 1967. All are in active Soviet service. These submarines are armed with eight SS-N-3 (and in some, SS-N-12) cruise missiles plus torpedo tubes. These submarines must surface to fire their missiles. The maximum effective range of the SS-N-3 missile in the antiship role is about 375 kilometers (250 nautical miles), however, the missile is capable of significantly longer aerodynamic flight. The submarine must rely on some outside source for targeting information when firing its missiles beyond visual/radar range of the submarine. For many years the ECHO II has been one of the primary anticarrier threats. Units of this class frequently deploy to the Mediterranean Sea.

**FOXTROT attack submarines**

## Attack Submarine (SS): FOXTROT class

| | |
|---|---|
| Displacement: | 2,000 tons surfaced |
| Length: | 91 meters (295 feet) |
| Propulsion: | Diesel-electric |
| Main Armament: | torpedo tubes |

The FOXTROT is a popular fleet-type attack submarine introduced in the late 1950s and still widely used. Eight have been provided to India, several to Libya, and two to Cuba. About 60 remain active in the Soviet Navy. The Soviets routinely deploy units of this class to the Mediterranean Sea and Indian Ocean and on occasion to the Caribbean.

**GOLF command and control submarine**

## Command and Control Submarine (SSAC): GOLF class

| | |
|---|---|
| Displacement: | 2,300 tons surfaced |
| Length: | 100 meters (328 feet) |
| Propulsion: | Diesel-electric |
| Main Armament: | torpedo tubes |

The GOLF class is a recent conversion of the GOLF I class SSB. The missiles have been removed and a variety of communication antennas have been installed, suggesting the submarines will perform some command, control, and communication function. The submarine probably retains its torpedo-firing capability. It's expected that more than one GOLF will be similarly converted.

91

**GOLF ballistic missile submarine**

## Ballistic Missile Submarine (SSB): GOLF I/II classes

| | |
|---|---|
| Displacement: | 2,300 tons surfaced |
| Length: | 100 meters (328 feet) |
| Propulsion: | Diesel-electric |
| Main Armament: | 3 SS-N-4 or 3 SS-N-5 SLBMs |
| | torpedo tubes |

Twenty-three GOLF diesel ballistic missile submarines (SSB) were built from 1958 to 1962, one of which accidentally sank in the mid-Pacific in 1967. The submarines were built to carry three SS-N-4 Submarine Launched Ballistic Missiles (SLBM). These SLBMs were launched while the submarine was surfaced and had an estimated range of over 600 kilometers (325 nautical miles). Many of these submarines were modified to the GOLF II configuration carrying the SS-N-5 SERB SLBM with estimated range of 1,300 kilometers (700 nautical miles), and can launch their missiles while submerged. About 15 units, mostly GOLF IIs, are still in active service with six of them based in the Baltic.

**GOLF III ballistic missile submarine**

## Ballistic Missile Submarine (SSB): GOLF III class

| | |
|---|---|
| Displacement: | 2,900 tons surfaced |
| Length: | 110 meters (360 feet) |
| Propulsion: | Diesel-electric |
| Main Armament: | 6 SS-N-8 SLBMs |
| | torpedo tubes |

The GOLF III is a one-of-a-kind conversion from a GOLF I SSB. It incorporates additional hull sections in the missile tube area and an elongated sail which encloses six SS-N-8 missiles. This unit was probably converted for missile test purposes. Another GOLF conversion, the single GOLF IV, was no doubt intended as a test platform for the SS-N-6 missile.

## Nuclear Powered Ballistic Missile Submarine (SSBN): HOTEL II/III classes

| | |
|---|---|
| Displacement: | 5,000 tons surfaced |
| Length: | 115 meters (377 feet) |
| Propulsion: | Nuclear |
| Main Armament: | 3 SS-N-5 SLBMs |
| | torpedo tubes |

Eight of the HOTEL SSBN class were completed from 1958 to 1962. Initially the submarines carried three surface launched SS-N-4 missiles. Their conversion to the HOTEL II configuration replaced the SS-N-4 with the submerged-launched SS-N-5. One HOTEL (now designated HOTEL III) has been modified to a missile test submarine for a later SLBM.

**INDIA Class SSAG**

## Auxiliary Submarine (SSAG): INDIA Class

| | |
|---|---|
| Displacement: | 3,000 tons surfaced |
| Length: | 105 meters (345) feet) |
| Propulsion: | Diesel-electric |
| Main Armament: | Probably torpedo tubes |

The INDIA is a search and rescue submarine and carries two submersible vehicles nested in wells aft of the sail.

## Cruise Missile Submarine (SSG): JULIETT class

| | |
|---|---|
| Displacement: | 3,000 tons surfaced |
| Length: | 90 meters (295 feet) |
| Propulsion: | Diesel-electric |
| Main Armament: | 4 SS-N-3 antiship missiles |
| | torpedo tubes |

Sixteen JULIETT submarines were built during the early 1960s. The JULIETT is fitted with four tubes for the SS-N-3 antiship cruise missile which is a surface-launched weapon of about 250nm range. As with the ECHO II class, over-the-horizon targeting must be accomplished with outside sources. All 16 submarines are believed to be in active service. Units are frequently deployed to the Mediterranean Sea.

## Auxiliary Submarine (SSAG): LIMA Class

The LIMA Class is a new small submarine probably intended for research purposes.

**NOVEMBER attack submarine**

## Nuclear Powered Attack Submarine (SSN): NOVEMBER class

| | |
|---|---|
| Displacement: | 4,500 tons surfaced |
| Length: | 110 meters (360 feet) |
| Propulsion: | Nuclear |
| Main Armament: | torpedo tubes |

The NOVEMBER SSN, the first Soviet nuclear powered submarine, became operational in 1959. Fourteen units were completed by 1965. One NOVEMBER sank in the eastern Atlantic in April of 1970 (pictured above, the crew was removed before sinking). The NOVEMBER class submarines are armed with torpedoes and, as most attack submarines, can also carry mines. Submarines of this class pioneered Soviet operations under the Arctic pack ice.

### Nuclear Powered Cruise Missile Submarine (SSGN): OSCAR Class

The initial unit of the OSCAR Class SSGN was launched in the spring of 1980 and is expected to join the fleet by early 1981. It is no doubt the largest general purpose submarine in the world. This ship will carry 20 to 30 cruise missiles of a new design (possibly the same type that is carried on the new nuclear powered missile cruiser, KIROV).

### Nuclear Powered Cruise Missile Submarine (SSGN): PAPA Class

This submarine is somewhat larger than a CHARLIE SSGN and might have been a prototype for that submarine's successor. Although in the Soviet inventory for a number of years it is believed that only one of this class was built. The PAP is estimated to carry eight SS-N-9 or SS-N-7 cruise missiles. (See photo following discription of CHARLIE I).

**ROMEO attack submarine**

### Attack Submarine (SS): ROMEO class

| | |
|---|---|
| Displacement: | 1,400 tons surfaced |
| Length: | 79 meters (262 feet) |
| Propulsion:. | Diesel-electric |
| Main Armament: | torpedo tubes |

About 20 ROMEO class submarines were completed between 1958 and 1961. Built along WHISKEY class lines, ROMEOs probably have improved ASW capabilities over the WHISKEY. Six of these submarines have been transferred to Egypt, two to Bulgaria, and a number have been built in China (PRC) and North Korea. The ROMEO class submarines have eight torpedo tubes and can launch mines as well as torpedoes.

TANGO attack submarine

## Attack Submarine (SS): TANGO class

| | |
|---|---|
| Displacement: | 3,000 tons surfaced |
| Length: | 90 meters (295 feet) |
| Propulsion: | Diesel-electric |
| Main Armament: | torpedo tubes (probably ASW missiles) |

The TANGO is a modern diesel-electric powered, torpedo-attack submarine. This submarine continues in series production and reflects the most modern diesel-electric technology. It has a long endurance when submerged and operates quietly on batteries. The first TANGO became operational in 1973, and a number of units have been constructed, demonstrating the Soviet Navy's continued interest in advanced diesel submarines. Units of this class frequently deploy to the Mediterranean.

## Nuclear Powered Ballistic Missile Submarine (SSBN): TYPHOON class

The initial unit of the TYPHOON Class was launched in the fall of 1980 and is expected to join the fleet sometime in 1981. Available information indicates this huge submarine is half again larger than the U.S. Navy's new OHIO Class SSBN in tonnage (the OHIO is about 18,000 tons submerged and carries 24 TRIDENT missiles). The missile this giant will carry probably will have better capabilities than the SS-N-18 (range over 4,000 nautical miles and MIRV capable) now embarked on the DELTA III Class.

VICTOR I attack submarine

### Nuclear Powered Attack Submarine (SSN): VICTOR I class

| | |
|---|---|
| Displacement: | 4,000 tons surfaced |
| Length: | 95 meters (311 feet) |
| Propulsion: | Nuclear, over 30 knots submerged |
| Main Armament: | torpedo tubes |

The first VICTOR class SSN was completed in 1967. This high-speed attack submarine was developed as a next generation to the NOVEMBER class, representing significant Soviet qualitative improvement in nuclear submarine design. The armament of the VICTOR consists of torpedoes and possibly antisubmarine missiles. This submarine class is one of the fastest in the world.

**VICTOR II attack submarine**

### Nuclear Powered Attack Submarine (SSN): VICTOR II class

| | |
|---|---|
| Displacement: | 4,500 tons surfaced |
| Length: | 100 meters (322 feet) |
| Propulsion: | Nuclear, over 30 knots submerged |
| Main Armament: | torpedo tubes and |
| | probably antisubmarine missiles |

These submarines represent an improved follow-on of the VICTOR I class. They are slightly larger than the VICTOR I and probably have improved weapons and sensor fits. These submarines probably carry a submerged launched antisubmarine missile system similar to our SUBROC. It is reported that the Soviets have produced even another variant of the VICTOR. In one form or another, the VICTORs continued to be built and are the "backbone" of the Soviets nuclear attack submarine force.

**WHISKEY attack submarine**

## Attack Submarine (SS): WHISKEY class

| | |
|---|---|
| Displacement: | 1,035 tons surfaced |
| Length: | 75 meters (246 feet) |
| Propulsion: | Diesel-electric |
| Main Armament: | torpedo tubes |

The design of the medium-range WHISKEY class SS was based extensively on later German World War II design concepts. Approximately 235 submarines of this class were built during the 1950s in what was the largest submarine construction program of the post-World War II period. A number of units remain in Soviet active and reserve service, with some 40 to 50 submarines serving in the navies of Albania, Bulgaria, China (PRC), Egypt, Indonesia, North Korea, Cuba, and Poland. WHISKEY submarines are armed with six torpedo tubes. The various deck guns mounted in early variants have been removed from the surviving units. Modifications include CANVAS BAG radar picket submarine (SSR), and the TWIN CYLINDER and LONG BIN surfaced launched missile variations (SSG) carrying the SS-N-3 antiship or tactical nuclear missiles.

**YANKEE ballistic missile submarine**

## Nuclear Powered Ballistic Submarine (SSBN): YANKEE I class

| | |
|---|---|
| Displacement: | 8,000 tons surfaced |
| Length: | 130 meters (426 feet) |
| Propulsion: | Nuclear |
| Main Armament: | 16 SS-N-6 Strategic SLBMs |
| | torpedo tubes |

The YANKEE I class, which became operational in 1968, was the first modern design SSBN in the Soviet Navy. A total of 34 submarines of this class was built. The YANKEE has 16 missile tubes for the SS-N-6 liquid fueled ballistic missile. There are three variants of the missile with ranges up to 2,950 kilometers (1,600 nautical miles). Some have MRV warheads. The SS-N-17 is a longer-range, solid fuel, more capable missile which is fitted in the YANKEE II variant of this class. To date only one YANKEE II has been so fitted. In order to keep within the limits of the SALT I agreement with the U.S., as each new DELTA SSBN joins the fleet, an older YANKEE I class SSBN has its missile tubes removed. These "de-fanged" YANKEEs are currently carried in the order-of-battle as YANKEE SSN.

## Attack Submarine (SS): ZULU class

| | |
|---|---|
| Displacement: | 1,950 tons surfaced |
| Length: | 90 meters (295 feet) |
| Propulsion: | Diesel-electric |
| Main Armament: | torpedo tubes (SSB version carries two SS-N-4 SLBMs in sail) |

About 26 ZULU class submarines were produced from 1952 to 1955. The ZULU is longer ranged than the WHISKEY class of the same period and is fitted with more torpedo tubes. Several modifications were made, including the ZULU V, armed with two SS-N-4 ballistic missiles, which made them the first submarines in the world to carry ballistic missiles. Six ZULU hulls were completed as, or converted to, SSBs, but only one unit remains so configured. The others reverted to SS status. ZULUs have been used in conjunction with research ships on extended oceanographic expeditions throughout the worlds oceans.

# AVIATION SHIPS

**KIEV aircraft carrier**

## Guided Missile V/STOL Aircraft Carrier (CVHG): KIEV* class

| | |
|---|---|
| Displacement: | 37,000 tons |
| Length: | 270 meters (900 feet) |
| Propulsion: | steam turbines, over 30 knots |
| Main Armament: | 4 twin SS-N-12 launchers |
| | 2 twin SA-N-3 SAM launchers (GOBLET) |
| | 2 twin SA-N-4 SAM launchers |
| | 1 twin SUW-N-1 ASW launcher |
| | 2 twin 76mm dual purpose (DP) gun mounts |
| | 8 single 30mm Gatling guns |
| Aircraft: | approx. 35 YAK-36 FORGER VTOL aircraft |
| | and KA-25 HORMONE helicopters |

The KIEV is the largest combatant class yet built in the Soviet Union. KIEV became operational in 1976, MINSK in 1978, a third unit is fitting out, and another is under construction. This ship is considered the first Soviet "aircraft carrier," with the flexibility to deploy a mix of fixed and rotary-wing aircraft for a number of missions. Weapons include eight surface-to-surface cruise missile tubes, two twin SA-N-3 and two SA-N-4 SAM launchers, two 76-mm twin gun mounts, and eight "Gatling" guns. This is the first class since the KYNDA class CG which carries reloads for its surface-to-surface missile system. For ASW the ship has a twin antisubmarine missile launcher, two antisubmarine rocket launchers, and torpedo tubes as well as hull-mounted and variable-depth sonars. The KIEV class features a starboard "island" superstructure and an angled flight deck. The lack of catapults and arresting gear limits the KIEV to operating helicopters and Vertical Short Take Off and Landing (VSTOL) aircraft. Aircraft observed aboard the class to date are the FORGER A and B as well as HORMONE A/B/C variants. It is estimated the ship can carry 35 to 40 aircraft depending on the mix of VSTOL aircraft and helicopters embarked. KIEV is based in the Northern Fleet while MINSK is based in the Pacific Ocean Fleet.

Ships of the class are: KIEV and MINSK.

## Nuclear Powered Guided Missile Cruiser (CHG): KIROV class

| | |
|---|---|
| Displacement: | 23,000 tons |
| Length: | 245 meters (810 feet) |
| Propulsion: | nuclear with fossil-fueled auxiliary, over 30 knots |
| Main Armament: | 20 new type cruise missiles |
| | 12 new type SAM launchers |
| | 2 twin SA-N-4 SAM launchers |
| | 2 twin SS-N-14 ASW missile launchers with reloads |
| | 2 single 100mm dual purpose gun mounts |
| | 8 single 30mm Gatling guns |
| Aircraft: | several HORMONE helicopters |
| | with elevator and hangar deck aft |

The KIROV is the Soviets' first nuclear powered surface warship. This ship had been under construction in Baltic Yard in Leningrad for a number of years and a second of the class will probably be launched within the year. After running sea trails in the Baltic through the summer of 1980 KIROV joined the Northern Fleet. This is the largest warship (other than aircraft carriers) built in the world since the end of World War II. Besides its large and varied weapons fit (which also includes torpedoes and ASW rockets) this ship is equipped with a vast array of electronics sensors and equipment including a new type large variable depth sonar, which is trailed from the stern door. The new cruise missiles are thought to be improvements over the SS-N-3/SS-N-12 family and the new SAM system may be a seaborne derivative of the ground based SA-X-10 missile system.

## Guided Missile Aviation Cruiser (CHG): MOSKVA* class

| | |
|---|---|
| Displacement: | 17,000 tons full load |
| Length: | 190 meters (623 feet) |
| Propulsion: | steam turbines, 30 knots |
| Main Armament: | 2 twin SA-N-3 SAM launchers (GOBLET) |
| | 1 twin SUW-N-1 ASW launcher |
| | 2 twin 57mm AA gun mounts |
| Aircraft: | 18 KA-25 HORMONE helicopters |

The MOSKVA and the LENINGRAD were completed in 1967 and 1968, respectively. The unique design of the ships includes a guided missile cruiser configuration forward and helicopter deck aft. There is a hangar deck below the flight deck which is serviced by two aircraft elevators. The MOSKVA class weapons suit includes twin antiaircraft and antisubmarine missile launchers, antisubmarine rockets, and torpedo tubes. The ships have hull-mounted and variable-depth sonars. They can carry about 18 HORMONE helicopters, with most or all normally configured for ASW. Both ships are home based in the Black Sea Fleet and operate regularly with the Mediterranean squadron.

Ships of the class are: MOSKVA and LENINGRAD.

## Guided Missile Cruiser (CG): KARA class

| | |
|---|---|
| Displacement: | 9,700 tons full load |
| Length: | 175 meters (574 feet) |
| Propulsion: | gas turbines, 32 knots |
| Main Armament: | 2 quad SS-N-14 ASW missile launchers |
| | (SILEX) (no reloads) |
| | 2 twin SA-N-3 SAM launchers (GOBLET) |
| | 2 twin SA-N-4 SAM launchers |
| | 2 twin 76mm DP gun mounts |
| | 4 single 30mm Gatling guns |
| Aircraft: | 1 KA-25 HORMONE helicopter |

The KARA is one of the newest of Soviet guided missile cruiser classes. This is a highly capable, heavily armed warship, first seen at sea in 1973. The KARA weapons consist of eight tubes for the SS-N-14 antisubmarine missile, ten torpedo tubes, and antisubmarine rocket launchers plus dual purpose guns and surface-to-air missiles. A helicopter hangar and platform are fitted aft. Seven ships of this class are currently operational, with construction of the class probably complete. One unit, the AZOV, is extensively modified aft and is estimated to be the test platform for a new SAM system, probably to be installed on one or more of the four new major combatant classes.

The ships of this class are: AZOV, KERCH, NIKOLAYEV, OCHAKOV, PETROPAVLOVSK, TALLIN and TASHKENT.

## Guided Missile Cruiser (CG): KRESTA I class

| | |
|---|---|
| Displacement: | 7,500 tons full load |
| Length: | 155 meters (508 feet) |
| Propulsion: | steam turbines, 32 knots |
| Main Armament: | 2 wtin SS-N-3 SSMs launches |
| | (no reloads) |
| | 2 twin SA-N-1 SAM launchers (GOA) |
| | 2 twin 57mm AA gun mounts |
| Aircraft: | 1 KA-25 HORMONE helicopter |

The KRESTA I cruiser is slightly smaller than the KRESTA II. It is a versatile and heavily armed ship with antiship cruise missile tubes, two antiaircraft missile launchers, guns, ten torpedo tubes, antisubmarine weapons, and a helicopter platform with hangar. The KRESTA I was the first Soviet combatant to have a helicopter hangar. Four units of this class were completed prior to development of the KRESTA II follow-on design. One ship has been fitted with four rapid-fire "Gatling" guns. The SS-N-3 surface-to-surface cruise missiles carried by this class are estimated to be capable of delivering either a nuclear or high explosive warhead over a distance of about 250nm. No reloads are provided on board for this weapon.

The ships of this class are: ADMIRAL ZOZULYA, SEVASTOPOL, VITSE ADMIRAL DROZD, and VLADIVOSTOK.

**KRESTA II guided missile cruiser**

## Guided Missile Cruiser (CG): KRESTA II class

| | |
|---|---|
| Displacement: | 7,600 tons full |
| Length: | 160 meters (524 feet) |
| Propulsion: | steam turbines, 32 knots |
| Main Armament: | 1 quad SS-N-14 ASW missile launchers (SILEX) (no reloads) |
| | 2 twin SA-N-3 SAM launchers (GOBLET) |
| | 2 twin 57mm AA gun mounts |
| Aircraft: | 1 KA-25 HORMONE helicopter |

The first KRESTA II cruiser became operational about 1970. These ships are armed with eight tubes for the 30nm range SS-N-14 antisubmarine missile, twin antiaircraft missiles launchers, four 57-mm AA and four "Gatling" antiaircraft guns, ten torpedo tubes, antisubmarine weapons, and a helicopter platform with hangar. Ten ships of this class are operational. Ships of this class are: ADMIRAL ISACHENKOV, ADMIRAL ISAKOV, ADMIRAL MAKAROV, ADMIRAL NAKHIMOV, ADMIRAL OKTYABR'SKIY, ADMIRAL YUMASHEV, KRONSHTADT, MARSHAL TIMOSHENKO, MARSHAL VOROSHILOV, and VASILY CHAPAYEV.

**KYNDA guided missile cruiser**

## Guided Missile Cruiser (CG): KYNDA class

| | |
|---|---|
| Displacement: | 5,500 tons full load |
| Length: | 140 meters (459 feet) |
| Propulsion: | steam turbine, 34 knots |
| Main Armament: | 2 quad SS-N-3 SSM launchers |
| | 1 twin SA-N-1 SAM launcher (GOA) |
| | 2 twin 76mm DP gun mounts |

The first of four KYNDA class cruisers appeared in 1962. When introduced, this missile cruiser class was unique in that it carried antiship missiles rather than antiaircraft missiles as the main battery. Antisubmarine rockets and torpedoes are also provided as well as a helicopter landing area (no hangar). The KYNDA is the only Soviet cruiser with reloads for the antiship missile launchers (eight reloads are carried in the superstructure). As in the KRESTA I, JULIETT and ECHO II class submarines, SS-N-3 surface-to-surface cruise missiles carried by this class of ship are estimated to be capable of delivering either a nuclear or high explosive warhead over a distance of about 250nm.

The ships of this class are: ADMIRAL FOKIN, ADMIRAL GOLOVKO, GROZNYY and VARYAG.

**SVERDLOV class cruiser**

## Light Cruiser (CL): SVERDLOV* class

| | |
|---|---|
| Displacement: | 17,000 tons full load |
| Length: | 210 meters (689 feet) |
| Propulsion: | steam turbines, 32 knots |
| Main Armament: | 12 6-inch (152mm) guns |
| | (4 triple turrets) except |
| | 6 guns in ADMIRAL SENYAVIN and |
| | 9 guns in ZHDANOV and DZERZHINSKIY |
| | 6 twin 100mm guns |
| | 16 twin 37mm guns |
| | torpedo tubes and mine rails |
| | SA-N-2 twin SAM launcher in DZERZHINSKIY |
| | (only ship so equipped) |
| | SA-N-4 SAM launcher in ADMIRAL SENYAVIN |
| | and ZHDANOV |

Fourteen of these large, light cruisers were built during the early 1950s. (Light cruisers are so designated due to gun size vice ship size, light = guns with less than an 8 inch bore.) Subsequently, one ship was stricken following use as a missile test platform and another was transferred to Indonesia (also later scrapped). In the early 1960s, one SVERDLOV, the DZERZHINSKIY, was converted to a guided missile cruiser (CG). Nine are considered still in commission.

Two SVERDLOVs, the ADMIRAL SENYAVIN and ZHDANOV, were converted to a command ship configuration in the early 1970s. These ships are fitted with staff accommodations and elaborate communications equipment. Some 152-mm guns were removed and helicopter facilities, an SA-N-4 SAM launcher, and several 30-mm antiaircraft guns were installed.

Other ships of this class are: ADMIRAL USHAKOV, ADMIRAL LAZAREV, ALEKSANDR NEVSKIY, ALEKSANDR SUVOROV, DMITRIY POZHARSKIY, MIKHAIL KUTUZOV, MURMANSK, and OKTYABR'SKAYA REVOLUTSIYA.

## Guided Missile Destroyer (DDG): SOVREMENNYY class

| | |
|---|---|
| Displacement: | 7,500 tons |
| Length: | 155 meters (510 feet) |
| Propulsion: | gas turbines |
| Main Armament: | unknown SSM system |
| | unknown SAM system |
| | unknown gun system |
| | 4 single 30mm Gatling guns |
| Aircraft: | 1 HORMONE helicopter |

The SOVREMENNYY is the initial unit of a new class missile destroyer which is expected to join the fleet in 1981. In conducted sea trials in the Baltic in the summer of 1980, but did not have most of its armament installed at that time. It has provisions to mount multiple cruise missile launchers either side of the bridge structure (these could possibley be the SS-N-9)); there are two deck openings which are thought to be for a new SAM system (possibley the seaborne version of the SA-X-11 ground based weapon); and what appears to be two deck areas prepared to receive gun mounts of 100mm caliber or larger. Torpedo tubes and ASW rockets are also installed. There is a helicopter deck with telescoping hanger capable of holding one HORMONE.

**KANIN guided missile destroyer**

## Guided Missile Destroyer (DDG): KANIN class

| | |
|---|---|
| Displacement: | 4,800 tons full load |
| Length: | 140 meters (460 feet) |
| Propulsion: | steam turbines, 35 knots |
| Main Armament: | 1 twin SA-N-1 SAM launcher |
| | 2 quad 57mm AA gun mounts |

The KANINs were originally KRUPNYY class guided missile destroyers and were subsequently converted. The KANIN class is primarily an antisubmarine ship with a fair antiaircraft capability. The ship design consists of the basic KRUPNYY destroyer hull and engineering plant armed with antiaircraft guns and missiles, ten antisubmarine torpedo tubes, antisubmarine rocket launchers, and a helicopter platform.

The ships of this class are: BOYKIY, DERZKIY, GNEVNYY, GORDYY, GREMYASHCHIY, UPORNYY, ZHGUCHIY and ZORKIY.

**KASHIN guided missile destroyer**

## Guided Missile Destroyer (DDG): KASHIN/MOD KASHIN classes

| | |
|---|---|
| Displacement: | 4,500 tons full load |
| Length: | 145 meters (476 feet) |
| Propulsion: | gas turbines, over 35 knots |
| Main Armament: | 2 twin SA-N-1 SAM launchers (GOA) |
| | 4 improved SS-N-2 SSMs (STYX) |
| | and 4 Gatling guns on MOD KASHIN |
| | 2 twin 76mm DP gun mounts |

The KASHIN was the world's first large gas-turbine powered warship. The ship's armament consists of two twin antiaircraft missile launchers, dual-purpose guns, five torpedo tubes, mine rails, antisubmarine rockets, and a helicopter landing pad (no hangar). Several ships of the MOD KASHIN class have been provided with improved antiair, antisubmarine, and antiship capabilities over the basic KASHIN class. Additionally, the MOD ships are armed with four launchers for SS-N-2 STYX type missiles and "Gatling" antiaircraft guns. Additional ships will probably be modified. Since the first unit was completed in 1962, 20 ships of the KASHIN class have been built. One KASHIN suffered an internal explosion and sank in the Black Sea in August 1974. Nineteen ships remain in the inventory. The Indian Navy ordered three ships of this class from Soviet shipbuilders to be delivered in the early 1980's.

**MOD KILDIN destroyer**

# Destroyer (DD): MOD KILDIN class

| | |
|---|---|
| Displacement: | 3,500 tons full load |
| Length: | 126 meters (413 feet) |
| Propulsion: | steam turbines, 34 knots |
| Main Armament: | 4 improved SS-N-2 SSMs |
| | (STYX) (no reloads) |
| | 2 twin 76mm DP gun mounts |
| | 2 quad 57mm AA gun mounts |

Three of the original four KILDIN class destroyers have undergone extensive modification. Their new armament includes four STYX-type missile tubes and two 76-mm twin gun mounts aft in place of the SS-N-1 missile launcher orginally installed. Four torpedo tubes are also provided. These ships were built on a KOTLIN hull plan.

The ships of this class are: NEULOVIMY, BEDOVYY, PROZORLIVY, NEUDERZHIMYY.

## Guided Missile Destroyer (DDG): KOTLIN class

| | |
|---|---|
| Displacement: | 3,600 tons full load |
| Length: | 127 meters (417 feet) |
| Propulsion: | steam turbine, 34 knots |
| Main Armament: | single twin SA-N-1 SAM launcher |
| | single twin 130mm DP gun mount |
| | single quad 45mm AA gun mount |

Nine KOTLIN class destroyers were converted to DDGs in the 1960s, with a single twin SA-N-1 SAM launcher installed in place of the after 130-mm mount. These ships retained five of their 21 inch torpedo tubes and have added two 12 barreled (or in two ships 16 barreled) ASW rocket launchers. One unit has had three quad 57-mm mounts and three have had 4 twin 30-mm guns installed. Eight of this class remain in the Soviet inventory, one was transferred to Poland in 1970.

Ships of this class are: BLAGORODNYY, BLESTYASHCHIY, BRAVYY, BURLIVYY, BYVALYY, DAL'NOVOSTOCHNYY KOMSOMOLETS, MOSKOVSKIY KOMSOMOLETS, NAKHODCHIVYY, NAPORISTYY, NASTOYCHIVYY, NESOKRUSHIMYY, PLAMENNYY, SKROMNYY, SKRYTNYY, SOZNATEL'NYY, SPESHNYY, SPOKOYNYY, SVEDUSHCHIY, SVETLYY, VESKIY, VDOKNOVENNYY, VLIYATEL'NYY, VOZBUZHDYENNYY, VOSMUSHCHYENNYY, VYDERZHANNYY, and VYZYVAYUSHCHIY.

KOTLIN destroyer

## Destroyer (DD): KOTLIN class

| | |
|---|---|
| Displacement: | 3,500 tons full load |
| Length: | 125 meters (410 feet) |
| Propulsion: | steam turbines, 34 knots |
| Main Armament: | 2 twin 130mm DP gun mounts |
| | 2 or 4 twin 25mm gun mounts (MOD KOTLIN) |
| | 4 quad 45mm AA gun mounts |
| | 2 6-barrel ASW rocket launchers (MOD KOTLIN) |

Twenty-seven of the fast, general purpose KOTLIN class destroyers were built during the 1950s. Nine of these have since been converted to KOTLIN class DDGs and a number were modernized to MOD KOTLIN status. The MOD version carry 2 or 4 twin 25-mm guns, two 6 barreled ASW rocket launchers and only five 21-inch torpedo tubes. No further conversions or modifications of the remaining standard KOTLIN DDs are anticipated. Although these ships possess heavy conventional and torpedo armament (ten tubes) plus two 12 barreled ASW rocket launchers, they have marginal antisubmarine and antiaircraft capabilities for modern threats. The orginial KOTLIN class DD armament consisted of 2 twin 130-mm guns, 4 quad 45-mm and four 25-mm AA guns, ten torpedo tubes, antisubmarine weapons, and mine rails. Most of the other ships of the class are still in active Soviet service.

Ships of this class are: KOMSOMOLETS UKRAINY, KRASNYY KAVKAZ, KRASNYY KRYM, OBRAZTSOVYY, ODARYENNYY, OGNEVOY, OTVAZHNYY, PROVORONYY, RESHITEL'NYY, SDERZHANNYY, SKORYY, SLAVNYY, SMELYY, SMETLIVYY, SMYSHLYENNYY, SOOBRAZITEL'NYY, SPOSOBNYY, STEREGUSHCHIY, STROGIY, and STROYNYY.

**SKORYY destroyer**

## Destroyer (DD): SKORYY class

| | |
|---|---|
| Displacement: | 3,200 tons full load |
| Length: | 125 meters (410 feet) |
| Propulsion: | steam turbines, 33 knots |
| Main Armament: | 2 twin 130mm DP gun mounts |

Seventy-two ships of the SKORYY class were completed from 1949 to 1953. This was the first post-World War II destroyer construction program and are numerically the largest destroyer class built in the Soviet Union. The SKORYY was armed originally with four 5.1-inch guns, two 85-mm AA guns, seven or eight 37-mm AA guns, and ten torpedo tubes plus mine rails, and antisubmarine weapons. The Modified SKORYY configurations received improved antiair and antisubmarine weapons. About 15 SKORYY units remain in service in the Soviet Navy with others in reserve. Although 16 SKORYYs have been transferred to Egypt, Poland, and Indonesia, only some Egyptian units are now active in foreign navies.

Ships of this class are: BESSMENNYY, BESSTRASHNYY, BEZUDERZHNYY, BUYNYY, OGNENNYY, OKRYLENNYY, OSTOROZHNYY, OSTRYY, OTCHANYANNYY, OTCHYETLIVYY, OTMENNYY, OTVETSTVENNYY, OZHESTOCHYENNYY, OZHIVLYENNYY, SERDITYY, SER'YEZNYY, SMOTRYASHCHIY, SOKRUSHITEL'NYY, SOLIDNYY, SOVERSHENNYY, STATNYY, STEPENNYY, STROYKIY, STREMITEL'NYY, SUROVYY, SVOBODNYY, VDUMCHIVYY, VNEZAPNYY, VNIMATEL'NYY, VOL'NYY, and VRAZUMITEL'NYY.

**KRIVAK missile frigate**

## Missile Frigate (FFG): KRIVAK I/II class

| | |
|---|---|
| Displacement: | 4,000 tons full load |
| Length: | 125 meters (410 feet) |
| Propulsion: | gas turbines, 31 knots |
| Main Armament: | 4 SS-N-14 ASW missiles |
| | 2 twin SA-N-4 SAM launchers |
| | 4 76mm AA guns (2 twin mounts) or |
| | 2 100mm DP guns (2 single mounts) |
| | ASW rockets |
| | torpedo tubes |
| | mine rails |

The KRIVAK frigates are among the most heavily armed of their type afloat. These are primarily antisubmarine ships with hull-mounted and variable-depth sonars, and ASW missiles, rockets and torpedo tubes. The first KRIVAK put to sea in 1970; a total of 30 units are operational with construction of additional ships continuing. KRIVAK I units have 76-mm dual purpose guns; KRIVAK II—100-mm dual purpose guns.

KRIVAK I—Ships of this class are: BDITEL'NYY, BODRYY, DEYATEL'NYY, DOBLESTNYY, DOSTOYNYY, DRUZHNYY, LENINGRADSKIY KOMSOMOLETS, LETUCHIY, RAZUMNYY, RAZYASHCHIY, RETIVYY, SIL'NYY, STOROZHEVOY, SVIREPYY, and ZHARKIY.

KRIVAK II—Ships of this class are: GROMKIY, GROZYASHCHIY, NEUKROTIMYY, PYLKIY, RAZITEL'NYY, REZKIY, and REZVYY.

**GRISHA light frigate**

## Light Frigte (FFL): GRISHA class

| | |
|---|---|
| Displacement: | 1,200 tons full load |
| Length: | 70 meters (235 feet) |
| Propulsion: | gas turbine/diesel, 30 knots |
| Main Armament: | GRISHA I—1 twin 57mm AA gun mount, |
| | 1 twin SA-N-4 SAM launcher, |
| | 4 torpedo tubes |
| | GRISHA II—2 twin 57mm AA gun mounts, |
| | 4 torpedo tubes |
| | GRISHA III—1 twin 57mm AA gun mount, |
| | 1 twin SA-N-4 SAM launcher, |
| | 1 30mm gatling gun, |
| | 4 torpedo tubes |

The three versions of the GRISHA class are primarily designed for coastal antisubmarine operations, but do operate with some regularity with the deployed squadrons on the high seas. The GRISHA II class WFFL is used exclusively by the marine border guards of the KGB. The GRISHA III, with the Gatling gun, has improved close-in air defense. All ships carry two 12-barreled ASW rocket launchers and depth changes as well as a hull-mounted sonar. Some units carry a dipping sonar similar to that used on HORMONE A helicopters. The latter are used with "sprint and drift" tactics, where the ship lay dead on the water while "dipping" (listening on the sonar) then sprints to a new position to "dip" again.

Ships of this class include: AMETIST, BRILLIANT, IZUMRUD, RUBIN, SAFFIR and ZHEMCHUG.

**KONI frigate**

## Frigate (FF): KONI class

| | |
|---|---|
| Displacement: | 2,000 tons full load |
| Length: | 95 meters (315 feet) |
| Propulsion: | gas turbine/diesel, 28 knots |
| Main Armament: | 1 twin SA-N-4 launcher |
| | 2 twin 76mm dual purpose guns |
| | 2 twin 30mm guns |

The KONI class frigate has only been recently introduced. Two units have been delivered to East Germany and one to Yugoslavia. Its armament (which also includes ASW rockets and depth charge rails) and sensors are basic with no new technology evident. This class of ship appears to be intended primarily for foreign users.

ZELENODOLSK is a ship of this class.

**PETYA II light frigate**

## Light Frigate (FFL): PETYA I/II classes

| | |
|---|---|
| Displacement: | 1,140 tons full load |
| Length: | 82 meters (269 feet) |
| Propulsion: | combination diesel/gas turbines, 29 knots |
| Main Armament: | 2 twin 76mm DP gun mounts |
| | 1 five-tube torpedo mounts |
| | and 2 ASW rocket launchers |
| | PETYA I has 4 smaller ASW rocket launchers |
| | and only 1 five-tube torpedo mount |

The PETYA class of light frigates is designed primarily for coastal defense, although they operate regularly in the Mediterranean and often in more distant areas. The older PETYA I units became operational in 1960. The improved PETYA II units have two sets of five 16 inch torpedo tubes and two antisubmarine rocket launchers. Some PETYA I's and PETYA II's have been modified to carry variable-depth sonar. About 65 PETYA's have been built, with some units transferred to foreign client states.

**MIRKA II light frigate**

## Light Frigate (FFL): MIRKA I/II classes

| | |
|---|---|
| Displacement: | 1,150 tons full load |
| Length: | 83 meters (272 feet) |
| Propulsion: | combination diesel/gas turbine, 30 knots |
| Main Armament: | 2 twin 76mm DP gun mounts |

The MIRKA class, similar to the PETYA class FFL, is a small fast combatant armed with 76-mm guns, torpedo tubes, and antisubmarine rocket launchers. Nine of about 20 MIRKAs built have two banks of five torpedo tubes and no ASW rocket launchers aft and are designated the MIRKA II class.

Ships of this class are: GANGULETS and IVAN SLADKOV.

**RIGA frigate**

## Frigate (FF): RIGA class

| | |
|---|---|
| Displacement: | 1,320 tons full load |
| Length: | 91 meters (298 feet) |
| Propulsion: | diesels, 28 knots |
| Main Armament: | 3 single 100mm DP gun mounts |
| | 2 twin 37mm AA gun mounts |
| | 1 three-tube torpedo mount |

An estimated 64 RIGA class frigates were built from 1952 through 1958. The approximately 35 units still active in the Soviet Navy have been given improved antisubmarine capabilities with the addition of ASW rocket launchers. Ships of this class have been transferred to Bulgaria, East Germany, Finland, and Indonesia.

Ships of this class are: ASTRAKHAN'SKIY KOMSOMOLETS, ARKHANGEL'SKIY KOMSOMOLETS, BARS, BARSUK, BOBR, BUYVOL, BYK, GEPARD, GIYENA, KOBCHIK, KOMSOMOLETS GRUZIY, KOMSOMOLETS LITVIY, KRASNODARSKIY KOMSOMOLETS, KUNITSA, LEV, LEOPARD, LISA, MEDVED', PANTERA, ROSMAKHA, SHAKAL, TIGR, TURMAN, VOLK, VORON, and YAGUAR.

# SMALL COMBATANTS

**NANUCHKA I guided missile patrol combatant**

## Guided Missile Patrol Combatant (PGG): NANUCHKA I/II classes

| | |
|---|---|
| Displacement: | 950 tons full load |
| Length: | 70 meters (229 feet) |
| Propulsion: | diesels, over 30 knots |
| Main Armament: | 6 SS-N-9 SSMs |
| | 1 twin SA-N-4 SAM launcher |
| | single twin 57mm AA guns |
| | (NANUCHKA I) |
| | single 76mm AA gun |
| | 1 30mm Gatling Gun |
| | (NANUCHKA III) |

The NANUCHKA I and III classes are the largest of the Soviet guided missile patrol combatants. The class was designed for improved endurance and better sea-keeping qualties than earlier missile craft. The NANUCHKA armament includes six SS-N-9 antiship cruise missiles with a range of about 60 nautical miles. Significant defensive weapons are also provided. The first NANUCHKA was completed in 1969; construction continues. The NANUCHKA II class, equipped with four SS-N-2 missiles, is the export version and has been delivered to India.

RADUGA is a ship of this class.

**OSA I guided missile attack boat (Egyptian Navy)**

## Missile Attack Boat (PTG): OSA I/II classes

| | |
|---|---|
| Displacement: | 240 tons full load |
| Length: | 40 meters (131 feet) |
| Propulsion: | diesels, 34 knots |
| Main Armament: | 4 SS-N-2 STYX SSMs |
| | 2 twin 30mm gun mounts |

The OSA is numerically, the largest class of missile attack boat in the Soviet Navy with approximately 120 units currently in inventory. OSA class missile boats are large follow-ons to the obsolete KOMARs. OSAs are fitted with four STYX-type (SS-N-2) antiship cruise missile tubes plus 30-mm AA guns. Indian-manned OSAs sank one Pakistani destroyer and severely damaged a second in the 1971 Indo-Pakistani War. They were also thought responsible for the sinking of several merchant ships. Over 100 of the OSA class missile boats have been transferred to other countries, including Bulgaria, China (PRC), Cuba, Egypt, Algeria, Libya, East Germany, India, Poland, Romania, Syria, Yugoslavia, Iraq, Finland, Algeria, Bulgaria, North Korea, and Somalia. The OSA II units have an improved, longer range SS-N-2 missile.

Ships of this class are: BRESTSKIY KOMSOMOLETS, MICHURINSKIY KOMSOMOLETS, TAMBOVSKIY KOMSOMOLETS, KIROVSKIY KOMSOMOLETS, KRONSHTADSKIY KOMSOMOLETS, and KOMSOMOLETS TATARSKIY.

# AMPHIBIOUS SHIPS

**IVAN ROGOV amphibious assault transport dock**

**Amphibious Assault Transport Dock (LPD): IVAN ROGOV\* class**

| | |
|---|---|
| Displacement: | 13,000 tons full load |
| Length: | 158 meters (520 feet) |
| Propulsion: | gas turbine, about 20 knots |
| Main Armament: | 1 twin 76mm DP gun mount |
| | 1 twin SA-N-4 SAM launcher |
| | 4 single 30mm gatling guns |
| | 1 122mm multiple barrage bombardment |
| | rocket launcher |

With the introduction of the IVAN ROGOV LPD in 1978, the Soviet Navy gained two new capabilities for its amphibious assault forces. First, the ROGOV has a floodable well deck that is intended to carry air cushion vehicles as well as conventional landing craft. The LEBED class medium landing craft (air cushion) (LCMA) vehicle has been deployed with ROGOV. A total of three can be carried in the well. Additionally, the ROGOV has a helicopter hangar and two landing decks. To date, the HORMONE is the only helicopter observed operating from ROGOV. It is estimated that IVAN ROGOV can lift a Soviet naval infantry battalion reinforced with one company of tanks and other combat support equipment or a total of approximately 550 troops, 30 armored personnel carriers, and 10 tanks. Included are bow doors and ramp for over the beach off loading as well as a roll-on/roll-off capability onto the weather deck and the tank decks forward of the well. This ship is by far the largest amphibious unit to join the Soviet Navy—more will undoubtedly follow. IVAN ROGOV is the only ship of this class.

## Amphibious Vehicle Landing Ship (LST): ALLIGATOR class

| | |
|---|---|
| Displacement: | 5,500 tons full load |
| Length: | 113 meters (371 feet) |
| Propulsion: | diesels, 16 knots |
| Main Armament: | single twin 57mm gun mount |
| | single twin arm shore bombardment |
| | rocket launcher (some units) |

The ALLIGATOR is a landing ship with a tank deck and bow doors as well as a stern ramp. LSTs are used to transport Naval Infantry units with their equipment and vehicles. These ships are used regularly on distant deployments to the Mediterranean, Indian Ocean and West Africa. Armament varies on a number of these ships. Some have 2 AS-N-5 quad SAM launchers; two have 2 twin 25-mm AA guns and several have 40 tube 122-mm shore bombardment rocket launchers. Fourteen of this class were built before production closed.

Ships of this class are: ALEKSANDR TORTSEV, DONETSKIY SHAKHTER, KRASNAYA PRESNYA, KRYMSKIY KOMSOMOLETS, NIKOLAY FIL'CHENKOV, NIKOLAY VILKOV, PYETR IL'ICHEV, SERGEY LAZO, TOMSKIY KOMSOMOLETS, VORONEZHKIY KOMSOMOLETS, and 50 LET SHEFSTVA VLKSM.

## Amphibious Vehicle Landing Ship (LST): ROPUCHA class

| | |
|---|---|
| Displacement: | 3,600 tons full load |
| Length: | 113 meters (371 feet) |
| Propulsion: | diesels, 16 knots |
| Main Armament: | 2 twin 57mm gun mounts |
| | some have 2 SA-N-5 quad SAM launchers |

The Polish built ROPUCHA class LSTs have a covered vehicle deck with both bow and stern doors. The newest of Soviet LSTs, it was designed to carry a balanced load of troops and vehicles. Like the ALLIGATORs, ships of this class often deploy with the Soviet Mediterranean, West African, and Indian Ocean Squadrons. The Soviets recently transferred one of these ships to the navy of South Yemen. About 11 remain in the Soviet order-of-battle.

**POLNOCNY medium amphibious assault landing ship**

**Medium Amphibious Assault Landing Ship (LSM): POLNOCNY class**

| | |
|---|---|
| Displacement: | 800 to 1,100 tons full load |
| Length: | 73 to 80 meters (240–265 feet) |
| Propulsion: | diesels, 18 knots |
| Main Armament: | 1 or 2 twin 30mm gun mounts |
| | 2 18-tube 140mm shore bombardment |
| | rocket launchers |
| | some have 4 SA-N-5 quad SAM launchers |

The POLNOCNYs are Polish-built medium landing ships with bow doors and a covered vehicle deck. They have been built in three variants, each of different length and displacement. About 50 ships are currently in the Soviet Navy with more than 20 in the Polish Navy. Other units have been transferred to Algeria, Egypt, Indonesia, India, Iraq, Somalia and South Yemen. Several variations exist within the general POLNOCNY class with different bridge configurations, armament, and payloads. Most ships are armed with 30-mm AA guns and multi-barrel shore bombardment rocket launchers.

# Appendix D. SOVIET AIRCRAFT DESCRIPTIONS

*The combat capabilities of Naval Aviation are one of the main in-
dicators of the striking power of our modern Navy. Naval Aviation has
become truly oceanic in nature, and it has been transformed into a most
important naval warfare resource.*

*Admiral of the Fleet of the Soviet Union*
*S.G. GORSHKOV*

This appendix provides basic descriptive data and
photographs of the more significant Soviet Naval
aircraft. Naval aviation comprises about eleven percent of the total Soviet combat aircraft inventory. It
has become a significant adjunct to the expanding
Soviet Naval structure. The fact that naval aviation
is receiving the new supersonic BACKFIRE bomber
at about the same rate as the Soviet Air Force, and
the growing carrier based elements, attests to the
relative high priority Soviet Naval aviation is receiving.

Arrangement: Aircraft are arranged alphabetically
by NATO code name.

Classification: The dimensions, characteristics,
and general information contained in the appendix
are approximate.

Designations: All aircraft names given in this
appendix are NATO code names: "B" names prefix
Bomber aircraft; "F" names prefix Fighter aircraft; "M" names prefix Miscellaneous aircraft, including maritime resonnaissance/patrol aircraft;
and "H" names prefix Helicopters. One-syllable
names denote propeller driven aircraft and two-
syllable names are used for jet aircraft. The Soviet
designation scheme, which uses letters derived from
the name(s) of the aircraft designer (e.g., MIG, TU,
KA) and sequential numbers, provides a universal
designation basis for Soviet aircraft.

In English we refer to the naval air arm as Soviet
Naval Aviation (SNA). In Russian it is called
AVIATSIYA VOYENNO-MORSKOGO FLOTA
(AVMF).

MAY patrol/antisubmarine aircraft

# STRIKE/BOMBER AIRCRAFT

**BACKFIRE strike bomber**

## BACKFIRE

| | |
|---|---|
| Length: | 42 meters (140 feet) |
| Wingspan: | swept, 24 meters (80 feet) |
| | extended, 34 meters (110 feet) |
| Engines: | 2 turbofan |
| Maximum Speed: | approx. 1,100 knots |

The BACKFIRE is currently the only Soviet bomber aircraft in production. Over 50 operational model BACKFIRE B aircraft are deployed in Soviet Naval Aviation. They can carry air-to-surface cruise missiles of the AS-4 type. The role for these supersonic variable-geometry (swing) wing bombers in SNA is missile strike against carrier task forces and similar high value targets as well as bombing and mining tasks. As additional aircraft are produced, reconnaissance and electronic warfare may be added missions of their roles. BACKFIREs, flown by Soviet Long-Range Aviation, are equipped with a tail turret (probably twin 23-mm guns). Some have been reported with external weapons racks for carrying mines or bombs. Although not counted under any SALT Treaty, the Soviets have agreed to limit production of this aircraft to a total of 30 per year in a related separate agreement.

## TU-16 BADGER

| | |
|---|---|
| Length: | 38 meters (125 feet) |
| Wingspan: | 33 meters (110 feet) |
| Gross Weight: | 170,000 lbs. |
| Engines: | 2 turbojets |
| Maximum Speed: | 540 knots |

The BADGER TU-16 twin-turbojet medium bomber is employed by Soviet Naval Aviation in antiship, reconnaissance, electronic warfare, and tanker roles. The BADGER is the most numerous aircraft type in Soviet Naval Aviation with currently over 400 in service. The early versions of this aircraft first entered naval service in the late 1950s, and the design has been extensively developed since that time. BADGER-C and -G variants are armed with stand-off missiles for antiship strike; one AS-2 or two AS-6 on the former and two AS-5 or AS-6 on the latter. BADGER A bombers, which carry up to 9 tons of gravity (free-fall) bombs, are probably employed primarily for training and mine laying. About 70 BADGER-A aircraft are configured as tankers for in-flight refueling of strike and reconnaissance aircraft. About 70 BADGERs are employed as specially configured reconnaissance and electronic variants. BADGERs also are flown by Soviet Long-Range Aviation and the air arms of China (PRC), Egypt, Indonesia, and Iraq. Most BADGERs have two or three twin 23-mm gun turrets.

## TU-95 BEAR D

| | |
|---|---|
| Length: | 45 meters (147 feet) |
| Wingspan: | 50 meters (165 feet) |
| Gross Weight: | 356,000 lbs. |
| Engines: | 4 turboprop (counter-rotating propellers) |
| Maximum Speed: | 450 knots |

The TU-95 BEARs are the largest Soviet Naval Aircraft. About 50 of the BEAR D variant are flown in the maritime surveilance/reconnaissance role. As an assist in resovling over-the-horizon targeting, high flying BEAR Ds can provide cruise missile guidance information to aircraft, surface ship, and submarine launch platforms. The BEAR D has an unrefueled range of approximately 15,000 kilometers (8,000 nautical miles). Naval BEARs have flown from bases in the Murmansk area around the North Cape, down the Norwegian Sea, and across the Atlantic Ocean, landing in Cuba or Guinea. BEAR Ds have also been deployed to Somalia, Angola, and Vietnam, with some having flown reconnaissance missions along the U.S. east coast. BEAR A, B, C, and E variants (The latter is a reconnaissance version) are flown by Soviet Long-Range Aviation. The BEAR B and C carry the AS-3 KANGAROO missile, which is capable of attacking sea targets and are occasionally exercised in maritime strike roles. Most BEARs are equipped with three twin 23-mm guns. The BEAR F is the naval antisubmarine warfare variant.

**BEAR F**

## TU-95 BEAR F

| | |
|---|---|
| Length: | 45 meters (147 feet) |
| Wingspan: | 50 meters (165 feet) |
| Gross Weight: | 380,000 lbs. |
| Engines: | 4 turboprop |
| Maximum Speed: | 450 knots |

The BEAR F is the Soviet's long range antisubmarine warfare aircraft. This variant of the TU-95 BEAR entered service prior to 1973 and is suited primarily for long range, antisubmarine warfare and open-ocean maritime operations. The aircraft's equipment includes sonobuoys, radar for submarine detection, and torpedoes and depth bombs for attack. BEAR Fs continue to enter the naval aviation inventory.

**BLINDER medium bomber**

## TU-22 BLINDER

| | |
|---|---|
| Length: | 40 meters (133 feet) |
| Wingspan: | 24 meters (80 feet) |
| Gross Weight: | 185,000 lbs. |
| Engines: | 2 turbojets |
| Maximum Speed: | 1,000 knots |

The TU-22 BLINDER twin-turbojet medium bomber is employed by the Soviet Navy in both attack and reconnaissance roles. There are about 50 BLINDER A aircraft in naval service which carry gravity bombs. A few BLINDER Cs are configured for reconnaissance. Armament includes a twin 23-mm gun tail turret. These aircraft have a supersonic dash capability. BLINDERs, including the BLINDER B, the AS-4 KITCHEN missile variant, are also flown by Soviet Long-Range Aviation as well as the air forces of Iraq and Libya.

**FORGER VTOL fighter/attack aircraft**

## YAK-36 FORGER

| | |
|---|---|
| Length: | 15 meters (50 feet) |
| Wingspan: | 7 meters (23 feet) |
| Gross Weight: | 22,000 lbs. |
| Engines: | 2 lift-only jets and 1 lift/cruise jet |
| Maximum Speed: | transonic |

The YAK-36 FORGER is a VTOL (Vertical Take-Off and Landing) aircraft first deployed in mid-1976 on the Soviet carrier KIEV. The aircraft uses both the lift-only and the lift/cruise engines in vertical flight and while transitioning into horizontal flight. The lift-only engines are shut down during normal flight. The FORGER's four wing stations are believed to be capable of mounting a variety of weapons including air-to-air missiles, rocket pods, machine guns, bombs, and tactical air-to-surface missiles, as well as auxiliary fuel tanks. While the exact role of FORGER A is unclear, it appears suitable for a wide range of missions such as air defense, close air support, reconnaissance, and antiship strike. The FORGER B is a two-seat (combat capable) trainer version of the FORGER. Although the FORGER's capabilities are less than most Western contemporary aircraft, it gives the Soviets a fixed-wing sea-based air capability where they had none before. New, more advanced ship-borne aircraft types will appear in the Soviet fleet during the 1980s.

**HAZE antisubmarine helicopter**

## MI-14 HAZE A

| | |
|---|---|
| Length (fuselage): | 18 meters (60 feet) |
| Rotor Diameter: | 21 meters (70 feet) |
| Gross Weight: | 24,000 lbs. |
| Engines: | 2 turboshaft jets |
| Maximum Speed: | 135 knots |

The HAZE A, an antisubmarine warfare helicopter, was adapted from the twin turbine MI-8 HIP transport helicopter including the adaption of the fuselage to a boat hull. The rotary wing aircraft has been observed with towed Magnetic Anomaly Detection and dipping sonar and has been operational since 1975. Over 50 of these new helicopters are believed to have entered operational service in the SNA. The HAZE A is the replacement for the shore-based HOUND ASW helicopters. In its present configuration, the HAZE is not suitable for regular operation from ships as its rotors and tail cannot be folded to facilitate storage. The HAZE is also in service with other Warsaw Pact countries.

**HORMONE    helicopter**

## KA-25 HORMONE

| | |
|---|---|
| Length (fuselage): | 10 meters (32 feet) |
| Rotor Diameter: | 16 meters (52 feet) |
| Gross Weight: | 16,000 lbs. |
| Engines: | 2 turboshafts |
| | (counter-rotating main rotors) |
| Maximum Speed: | 130 knots |

The HORMONE is the Soviet Navy's standard shipboard helicopter. It is embarked in the KRESTA I and II, and KARA classes of missile cruisers, the MOSKVA and KIEV classes of aviation ships, the IVAN ROGOV class landing ship, the BEREZINA class replenishment ship, and most, if not all, the four new warship classes. The helicopters are configured for antisubmarine warfare (HORMONE A), missile targeting (HORMONE B), or for utility funtions (HORMONE C). HORMONE B helicopers are embarked in ships with antiship cruise missiles. About 200 HORMONEs are currently active in the Soviet Navy. Distinctive features of ungainly looking helicoper are a chin-mounted radome, triple tails, and two counter-rotating rotors. The HORMONE A has an internal weapons bay for torpedoes or depth charges and carries sonobuoys, dipping sonar, and an optical sensor. The HORMONE C has serveral variations including search and rescue, and transport and vertical replenishment.

**HOUND antisubmarine helicopter**

## MI-4 HOUND

| | |
|---|---|
| Length: | 17 meters (55 feet) |
| Rotor Diameter: | 21 meters (69 feet) |
| Gross Weight: | 17,200 lbs. |
| Engines: | 1 piston engine |
| Maximum Speed: | 115 knots |

The HOUND helicopter has been in Soviet military service since the early 1950s, although it was not operational in the Navy until 1959. They have chin-mounted radar, dipping sonar, and a towed magnetic detector. The HOUND is currently being phased out in favor of the HAZE. In addition to the HOUNDs in the Soviet military service, many are used commercially. Several foreign countries have HOUNDs in their military and commercial air services.

## BE-12 MAIL

| | |
|---|---|
| Length: | 30 meters (99 feet) |
| Wingspan: | 29 meters (97 feet) |
| Gross Weight: | 65,000 lbs. |
| Engines: | 2 turboprops |
| Maximum Speed: | 330 knots |

Soviet Naval Aviation operates these amphibious aircraft in maritime reconnaissance and antisubmarine warfare roles. The MAIL has distinctive gull-shaped wings, an elongated radar dome nose, and a MAD antenna protruding from the tail. Its weapons are carried on underwing pylons and in a weapons bay in the after section of the hull. Torpedoes, mines, or depth charges can be carried.

## IL-38 MAY

| | |
|---|---|
| Length: | 36 meters (118 feet) |
| Wingspan: | 37 meters (123 feet) |
| Gross Weight: | 141,000 lbs. |
| Engines: | 4 turboprops |
| Cruise Speed: | 340 knots |

Entering service in 1968, the MAY is used primarily for open ocean patrol and antisubmarine warfare. The aircraft was adapted from a commercial aircraft design (the IL-18 COOT) in the same manner that the U.S. Navy P-3 ORION was developed from the commercial ELECTRA aircraft. It closely resembles the P-3. The MAY has a radome under the forward fuselage and a MAD antenna protruding from the tail. ASW torpedoes are carried in an internal weapons bay. The Soviet aircraft has expendable sonobuoys and nonacoustic sensors, as well as a computerized tactical evaluation capability. Endurance is reported to be 12 hours at a patrol speed of about 220 knots. These aircraft have been deployed outside the Soviet Union on a number of occasions over the last several years, mainly to Aden, where they flew surveillance on U.S. naval forces operating in the Arabian Sea. MAYs are also flown by the Indian Air Force. This type does not appear to be under construction any longer.

# Appendix E. MISSILE GUIDE

| Air-to-Surface Missile | NATO Code Name | Range | Platforms |
|---|---|---|---|
| AS-2 | KIPPER | About 100nm | BADGER C/G |
| AS-3 | KANGAROO | 200–300nm | BEAR B/C |
| AS-4 | KITCHEN | 150–250nm | BLINDER B, BACKFIRE |
| AS-5 | KELT | About 100nm | BADGER G |
| AS-6 | KINGFISH | 150–250nm | BADGER C/G |

**Surface-to-Air**

| | | | |
|---|---|---|---|
| SA-N-1 | | About 10nm | KRESTA I, KYNDA, KANIN, KASHIN, KOTLIN |
| SA-N-2 | | About 30nm | DZERZHINSKIY (SVERDLOV class) |
| SA-N-3 | | About 30nm | KIEV, MOSKVA, KARA, KRESTA II |
| SA-N-4 | | About 8nm | KIEV, KARA, KIROV, SVERDLOV, KONI, GRISHA I/III, KRIVAK I/II, NANUCHKA, SARANCHA, IVAN ROGOV, BEREZINA |
| SA-N-5 | | About 3nm | ROPUCHA, POLNOCNY, some AGIs |

**Surface (or Sub-Surface)
-to-Surface
(or Sub-Surface)**

| | | | |
|---|---|---|---|
| SS-N-1 | SCRUBBER | About 100nm | KILDEN, KRUPNYY |
| SS-N-2 | STYX | About 25nm (SSM) | OSA I, KOMAR, NANUCHKA II, OSA I |
| SS-N-2 (Imp) | STYX (Improved) | About 40nm (SSM) | OSA II, MOD KASHIN, MOD KILDEN, MATKA, TARANTUL |
| SS-N-3b | SEPAL | About 250nm | KRESTA I, KYNDA, |
| SS-N-3c | SHADDOCK | (SSM) | ECHO I/II, JULIETT, WHISKEY Conversion |
| SS-N-4 | SARK | About 350nm (SLBM) | GOLF, HOTEL, ZULU V |
| SS-N-5 | SERB | About 700nm (SLBM | GOLF II, HOTEL II |
| SS-N-6 | SAWFLY | 1600nm (SLBM) | GOLF IV (Test Platform), YANKEE I |

| Missile | NATO Code Name | Range/Type | Platforms |
|---------|----------------|------------|-----------|
| SS-N-7 | | About 30nm (SSM) | CHARLIE I |
| SS-N-8 | | 4000nm + (SLBM) | DELTA I/II, GOLF III |
| SS-N-9 | SIREN | About 60nm (SSM) | NANUCHKA, SARANCHA, CHARLIE II, PAPA |
| SS-N-10 | cancelled designator | | |
| SS-N-11 | cancelled designator | | |
| SS-N-12 | | About 300nm (SSM) | KIEV, ECHO II |
| SS-NX-13 | | (SLBM) | Experimental, inactive |
| SS-N-14 | SILEX | About 25nm (ASW) | KARA, KIROV, KRESTA II, KRIVAK I/II |
| SS-N-15 | | Short Range (ASW) | Newer classes of submarines |
| SS-NX-16 | | Short Range (ASW) | Newer classes of submarines |
| SS-N-17 | | 1600nm + (SLBM) | YANKEE II |
| SS-N-18 | | About 5000nm (SLBM) | DELTA III |
| SUW-N-1 | | Short (ASW) | KIEV, MOSKVA |

A Soviet intelligence collector (AGI) closes on the stern of a U.S. aircraft carrier while observing flight operations in the Mediterranean Sea. Some of the larger Soviet AGIs are armed.

# GLOSSARY

**NOTE:** Definition of larger ship type designators such as SSBN, SS, CG, DDG, FEL, CVHG, LSM, LPD, etc. may be found in Appendix B and Appendix C.

| | |
|---|---|
| AAW | Antiair Warfare |
| AGI | Intelligence collection ship |
| AOR | Replenishment oiler |
| AS-(number) | U.S. designation for Soviet air-to-surface missile (see App. E) |
| ASUW | Antisurface Warfare |
| ASW | Antisubmarine Warfare |
| C$^3$ | Command, Control and Communications |
| CINC | Commander-in-Chief |
| CTOL | Conventional Take-Off and Landing (aircraft) |
| ELINT | Electronic Intelligence |
| Gatling gun | a generic term for a multibarrel machine gun |
| ICBM | Intercontinental Ballistic Missile |
| MIRV | Multiple Independently Targeted Re-entry Vehicle |
| mm | millimeters |
| MRV | Multiple Re-entry Vehicle |
| NATO | North Atlantic Treaty Organization |
| nm | nautical miles (equals 6,079.115 ft.) |
| PCS | submarine chaser |
| PCSH | Submarine chaser (Hydrofoil) |
| PG | Gunboat |
| PTH | Torpedo boat (Hydrofoil) |
| PTL | Small Torpedo boat |
| RO/RO | Roll-on/Roll-off |
| SA-N-(number) | U.S. designation for Soviet naval surface-to-air missile (see App. E) |
| SAM | Surface-to-Air Missile |
| SESS | Space Event Support Ship |
| SLBM | Submarine-Launched Ballistic Missile |
| SLOC | Sea Lines of communication |
| SNA | Soviet Naval Aviation |
| SS-N-(number) | U.S. designation for Soviet naval surface-to-surface or sub-marine-to-surface missile (see App. E) |
| VSTOL | Vertical and Short Take-Off and Landing (aircraft) |
| VTOL | Vertical Take-Off and Landing (aircraft) |
| WIG | Wing-in-ground effect (aircraft) |

# Index

ARKTIKA AGBN

YERMAK AGB

135 m

DUBNA AOR

UDA AOR

130m    12000 t

122 m    7000 t

ABKHAZIYA AGOR

124 m    7000 t

DESNA AGE

SIBIR AGE

PRIMORYE AGI

OKEAN AGI

TOMBA AG

UGRA AS

DON AS

NEPA ASR

PRUT (MOD) ASR